Welcome

Your Guide to
O GAUGE RAILWAY MODELLING
including the larger scales

Welcome to this, the latest addition to our Peco Modellers' Library of publications intended to encourage and advise on all aspects of railway modelling. If you're reading this, then you have probably made the decision to embark on a model railway project in O gauge. Whether you are a beginner, with little previous knowledge, or a returnee to the hobby during retirement, you will find this book a great introduction to the topic, guiding you through the key decisions that you will need to make – such as choosing between sectional and flexible track systems as appropriate to your scheme, and whether to adopt analogue or digital control.

British O gauge is supported by a large number of specialist suppliers that produce countless kits and accessories. Whilst this is a tremendous benefit to the would-be O gauge modeller, the huge array of products on offer, not to mention the different wheel and track standards that O gauge covers, can be rather overwhelming to navigate – particularly for new entrants to the hobby.

Therefore, we have devoted this publication to providing lots of ideas and suggestions on how to get started, including an overview of the commercial support, and an insight into the history of proprietary British O. We also take a look at the larger scales – namely Gauge 1 and Gauge 3, including live steam!

Many aspects of model making in O gauge are common with the smaller scales (including OO), such as general layout wiring principles, baseboard construction and the creation of scenery and landscapes. These topics are extensively covered in our earlier Peco Modellers' Library title, *Your Guide to Railway Modelling & Layout Construction*, and also in our ever popular series of Shows You How booklets, so we have not repeated detailed accounts of such methods and materials in this book. There are, nevertheless, over 30 pages of easy-going modelling projects to whet your appetite, whilst the rest of the book focuses on the many questions and initial steps you need to consider in order to integrate this wonderful and creative hobby successfully into your lifestyle.

Large scale railway modelling is a 'broad church' offering something for everyone. We are sure that, regardless of what interests you in terms of era or prototype, you will find something in the following pages to inspire you and set you on a path to creating a system to be proud of – and one that will provide you with many hours of enjoyment and fulfilment.

Steve Flint
Editor

Below
After spending many years modelling in N gauge, Chris Thorp made the jump to O when an attic space measuring 20' x 11' became available. *Glen Nevis* – Chris's second O gauge layout to occupy this space – recalls the West Highlands of Scotland in the BR blue era. *Photo: Derek Shore*

Editor & Photographer
Steve Flint

Production Editor
Tim Rayner

Features Writer & Photographer
Craig Tiley

Editorial Assistant
Julie Newbery

Art Director
Adrian Stickland

Additional Photography
Andrew Burnham, Jolyon Sargent,
Derek Shore, Len Weal,
Brian Monaghan, Paul Bason

Graphic Illustration
Brian Meredith, Dave Clements,
Gary Bickley, Steve Croucher
and David Malton

Modelmakers
David Malton, Andrew Beard and
Ian Thompson

General & Advertisement Manager
John King

Advertisement Assistants
Sue Davis and Nicole Charlton

Direct Subscriptions
Alicia Knight

Chairman
C M Pritchard

Editorial Office Telephone
01297 20580

ISBN 978-0-900586-57-6

Distribution to the model trade, direct subscriptions
(Home & Overseas) Pritchard Patent Product Co Ltd
(address and telephone as below).

Distribution to the newsagency trade (Home &
Overseas) Marketforce UK, 2nd Floor, 5 Churchill Place,
Canary Wharf, London E14 5HU.

Printed by
William Gibbons & Sons Ltd., P.O.Box 103,
26 Planetary Road, Willenhall, West Midlands
WV13 3XT.

Peco Publications & Publicity Ltd,
Beer, Seaton, Devon, EX12 3NA, England.
Telephone: 01297 20580 Fax 01297 20229
Website: www.peco-uk.com
Email: railway-modeller@btconnect.com

Contents

13

38

Introduction

The appeal of O gauge and the larger scales

Many seasoned modellers – particularly working in the smaller scales such as N and OO – find that the idea of modelling in O gauge (or even Gauges 1 and 3) holds an enduring appeal. This can perhaps be attributed to the undeniable physical presence that these larger scale models possess; even a four-wheel wagon exudes a sense of weight and volume that is seldom conveyed in the smaller scales. For some, the appeal may be nostalgia driven – an O gauge project perhaps rekindling memories of Hornby O gauge tinplate as a child.

Working in a larger scale also opens up the potential for modelling levels of detail and surface textures that are not otherwise possible, or indeed suited to 4mm and 2mm scales, and this in itself can present an attractive proposition. Many modellers also find working in a larger scale to be more straightforward; models and kit compo-

nents are bigger and therefore easier to handle, whilst detail work is often found to be less fiddly.

Large scale overview

The technical specifications for gauges O, 1 and 3 are covered later in this publication, but suffice to say at the outset that; British O gauge represents 1:43 scale with models running on 32mm gauge track (nearly twice the

Above
The sight of lengthy express passenger trains running at speed through an expansive landscape is impressive in any scale, but especially so in O. A model of the prototype Deltic is seen on *The Summit*, a layout by Yeovil MRG.

Right
A visual comparison of scales with 64xx 0-6-0PTs in N (Graham Farish), OO (Bachmann) and O (Dapol).

Far left
Arun Quay by Gordon and Maggie Gravett is an excellent example of the high level of scenic detailing that can be achieved in 7mm scale. *Photo: Gordon Gravett*

Left
This 7mm GWR clerestory coach model produced ready-to-run by Lee Marsh Model Co. incorporates exquisite interior detailing.

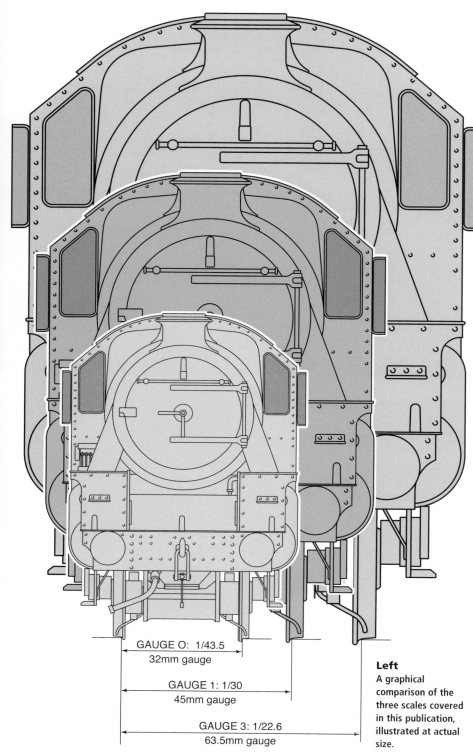

GAUGE O: 1/43.5
32mm gauge

GAUGE 1: 1/30
45mm gauge

GAUGE 3: 1/22.6
63.5mm gauge

Left
A graphical comparison of the three scales covered in this publication, illustrated at actual size.

size of OO, which is 1:76 scale on 16.5mm track); Gauge 1 is nominally 1:32 scale on 45mm track, whilst Gauge 3 uses a scale ratio of 1:22.6 and a track gauge of 63.5mm.

O gauge is regarded by many as the largest practical scale for use indoors at home (although as we shall see later on, there are exceptions to this!). Commercial support is available through many of the same channels and retailers that stock the smaller scales, such as OO and N. The scale is supported by a prodigious amount of ready-to-run equipment, together with proprietary track systems (including Peco), together with countless kits and accessories. Control options mirror those for the smaller scales, with both 12v DC analogue and 16v AC digital options being well supported for O gauge applications.

Moving up from O gauge the next option is **Gauge 1**, which can be regarded as the largest scale adopted by modellers who wish to replicate a complete railway with buildings and scenery, rather than individual models of locomotives or trains (although, once again there are exceptions). As such Gauge 1 straddles the boundary between what can be termed as railway modelling and miniature engineering. Often developed as outdoor or garden-based systems, Gauge 1 is popular with those concerned primarily with locomotives and rolling stock, including live steam. However, commercial support is not as extensive in comparison to O gauge, with Gauge 1 models, kits and accessories only stocked by specialist and garden railway suppliers. There are a number of locomotives and rolling stock models available ready-to-run in Gauge 1, together with proprietary track from Peco, but modelling in this scale will almost certainly require recourse to kit- or scratchbuilding for greater variety to be introduced, or for the modelling of the scenic details.

Gauge 3 is almost certainly the largest railway modelling scale that can use electric motor propulsion. However, whereas gauges O and 1 can use track power, Gauge 3 models are usually battery-powered, operated by radio control. Live steam is also a popular option in this scale; in fact Gauge 3 was historically very much the domain of the model engineer who wanted to run live steam (or gas-fired radio-controlled) models in a garden setting, but the availability of affordable electric locomotives in more recent times has brought the scale into the traditional railway modelling arena.

Modelling in Gauge 3 is quite a specialised discipline,

with a limited level of commercial support available primarily through garden railway retailers. However, an advantage of the 1:22.6 scale ratio used is that it is compatible with the huges ranges of G scale products (that uses a scale ratio of 1:22.5) such as LGB, including buildings, lineside accessories and figures.

Outdoor and garden railway systems

In the summer months, the prospect of running trains in the garden can be very appealing, it also presenting the opportunity to share your hobby with family and friends in a convivial outdoor setting. All of the aforementioned large scales are also particularly well suited to outdoor use. Indeed, if you are intent on running lengthy passenger trains hauled by express steam locomotives, but live in an average-sized family home, then an outdoor system is likely to be the only viable option to accommodate the train lengths and track radii required. Naturally, if live-steam is adopted as the control method of choice, then an outdoor location presents the only practical solution.

Whilst successful outdoor systems in the smaller scales (such as OO) have been completed over the years, O gauge is still regarded as the smallest practical scale for running in the garden. The larger actual size and greater weight of the locomotives and rolling stock help to ensure stable running can be maintained – even if there is a slight breeze, or small amounts of debris between the sleepers.

The trackwork itself is, in the larger scales, also of a more robust construction, with a deeper sleeper base and heavier rail section – meaning that it is much more resilliant to the ravages of the British weather. A further consideration is that, from a visual standpoint, the larger the scale, the better the models 'sit' against the backdrop of a garden environment, with grass lawns, flower beds and hedges.

Next steps

This introduction has provided a very brief overview of the scales and key topics covered in this volume. The information in the following chapters will provide the guidance you need to start you off in the right direction, whether that be an indoor compact O gauge industrial scheme controlled using DCC, or an expansive outdoor Gauge 1 main line continuous run with live-steam models.

However, as with all facets of railway modelling, there are no hard and fast rules and it is ultimately down to the ingenuity and imagination of the individual to succeed with creating a satisfying model in one of the larger scales.

Above left
Ready-to-run Gauge 1 models have been produced over the years, such as this Stanier 5MT 4-6-0 by Bachmann Brassworks.

Above right
St Ives, the classic GWR branch line terminus, modelled in Gauge 3 – all 88' of it! The impressive layout is the work of the late Michael Heaven and his friends.

Below
The larger scales are a popular choice for those wishing to take their modelling outdoors. *Combe Down* is a live steam Gauge 1 garden system by father and son team, Don and John Froud.

A history of British O

The cradle of the O gauge trains we all recognise today was Germany, and the stork – so to speak – was Märklin, a name still very much part of the continental model railway scene. For the 1891 toy fair in Leipzig it introduced a range of toy trains – 'scale' model railways were still far in the future – in three sizes: I, II and III. Gauge I was around 48mm, II was 54mm and III 75mm. Shortly thereafter, Märklin added items to a narrower gauge, 35mm, having seen what the more 'cottage industry' end of the market was achieving. The only logical designation was 0; purists still use this definition today, but it is generally better understood as O. (When in 1938 Hornby introduced its 'Dublo' range, the implicit contraction of 'double-oh' cemented the terminology as 'OhOh', thus giving 'gauge oh' legitimacy.)

The other players in the market, such as Bing, were slow to settle to Märklin's definitions, but by 1895 the terminology was accepted and understood. By 1900 the companies had secured a major segment of the toy market; in addition to lettering up German-outline models for overseas sales such as in the USA and Britain, firms such as Märklin and Bing created models to commissioners' specifications, the best-known of which in the UK was W J Bassett-Lowke.

Bassett-Lowke's engineering background, and his connections with minimum (ie 15") and miniature railway pioneers such as Henry Greenly, meant that he was active in many railway areas, not least the smallest model scale then in production, O. His needs for expansion meant that several premises in and around his base town of Northampton were acquired, plus a showroom in High Holborn in London, which was to remain a magnet for enthusiasts for decades. As an indication of his range, the 1910 catalogue ran to over 470 pages. His chief suppliers, Bing and Carette, received annual orders, normally in time for the Christmas rush. This was, of course, to become an impossibility after August 1914, when the outbreak of the Great War changed the model railway industry forever…

Bassett-Lowke had spent the war years engaged in munitions work, as

Left
A Märklin Gauge 1 electric-powered three-rail 0-4-0, circa 1900.
Photo: Vectis Auctions/ Pat Hammond Collection

Above
Clockwork propulsion was still popular in the 1950s, such as this sturdy 0-4-0T.
Photo: SAS Auctions/ Pat Hammond Collection

Above
By the second decade of the 20th century, locomotives had a closer to scale appearance. This is a 1924 Bing model of a Great Northern D1 4-4-0. *Photo: Pat Hammond Collection*

Right
The Gresley A3 No.4472 was a popular subject for modelling; this is a Bassett-Lowke clockwork model of 1933. *Photo: Vectis Auctions/Pat Hammond Collection*

Right
Top-end craftsmen working in O gauge included J S Beeson (1906 – 1990), whose GER E4 2-4-0, built in the mid-1930s, was part of the collection of the Peco founder Sydney Pritchard.

Below
By the late 1930s, two-rail was gaining popularity, such as this Bonds LMS 3F 0-6-0T of 1938. *Photo: Lacy, Scott & Knight/Pat Hammond Collection*

Below right
A Hornby Type 51 clockwork 0-4-0 of 1954, with the familiar red packaging. *Photo: Lacy, Scott & Knight/ Pat Hammond Collection*

had the world-famous Binns Road, Liverpool factory of Frank Hornby, who had, like Bassett-Lowke, become a household name thanks to his Meccano construction sets. With strident anti-German feeling post-war, Hornby seized the opportunity to enter an arena once dominated by products made in Nürnberg: the first train sets to bear his name were brought to market in 1920, at around the time that Bassett-Lowke was making tentative steps into the next smallest size of model trains – OO.

Hornby trains quickly became established as the chief brand for British O gauge, aided no doubt by the regular and enthu-

siastic promotion of the brand in the *Meccano Magazine* and other contemporary publications.

The growing success and popularity of OO had, by the mid 1930s, given Hornby food for thought. Trix – manufactured in the UK by Bassett-Lowke – had proved the technology could work, so the Dublo system was launched. The tinplate O gauge line was kept going through another world war, but it was clear which way the wind was blowing.

By the end of the 1950s Hornby O gauge had all but ceased to be, of interest only to collectors – at least for the tinplate product lines.

Model or toy?

The **Big Big Train**. With an 'O' gauge loco 14" long—authentic in detail and scale. It's battery powered and it runs on a tough polypropylene track. So it's safe, simple and very much an out-door type. The track is pliable and takes the ups and downs of a garden layout in its stride. And rain can't harm it. A fine model by any standards. But also a marvellous toy for very young children.

Trip switch gives auto-reverse. Clip this special trip switch on one side of the track and it stops the loco. Clip it on the other side, it puts the loco into reverse. This means the layout need not join up in a circle or an oval but can be laid end to end.

The **Big Big Train** comes in 2 sets. Loco, 4 trucks, 2 switches and 18 ft track for 99/6. Or Loco, 2 trucks and 12 ft circular track 69/6. Extra track, locos, trucks and switches are available.

THE BIG BIG TRAIN
Tri-ang PRODUCTS
ROVEX SCALE MODELS LTD · WESTWOOD · MARGATE · KENT

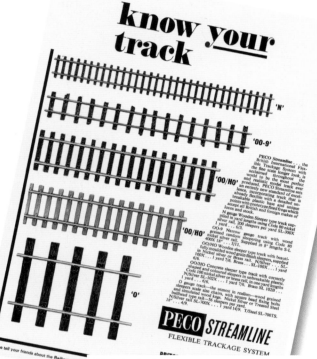

know your track

PECO Streamline ... the British International Fine-scale Trackage System with acclaimed throughout the fine scale prototype look is world to be the most perfect and realistic model track ever produced. PECO Streamline an entirely new standard of excel- sets ience, incorporating track that is already flexible with a detailed un- breakable plastic base and unique points with prototype/fixed frogs which accept all Bristol/type and foreign makes of locos and stock.

N gauge Wooden Sleeper type track sup- plied in yard lengths using Code 80 nickel silver rail, 200 sleepers per yard SL-300X
1 yard ... 6/3.
00-9 — Narrow gauge track with wood grained random sleepering using Code 80 nickel silver rail. Supplied in 8' lengths S-L 400X 18" ... 3/11.
00/HO Wooden sleeper type track with beauti- fully moulded wood grain finish sleepers, supplied in Nickel silver or Brass rail. N/Silver ... SL-100X ... 1 yard 7/6. Brass ... SL-100X ... 1 yard 6/6.
00/HO Concrete sleeper type track with correctly shaped and coloured sleepers in unbreakable plastic Code 100 nickel silver or brass rail, in one yard lengths. N/Silver SL-102X ... 1 yard 7/6. Brass SL-102 6/6 ... 1 yard.
O gauge track—the utmost in realism—wood grained sleepers to scale size chairs, with square head fixing bolts and simulated wood spikes, at kegs. Nickel Silver or Treated Steel bullhead type rail—56 sleepers per yard. N/Silver type rail SL-700X ... 1 yard 14/9. T/Steel SL-700TS. 18" ... 4/9.

PECO STREAMLINE
FLEXIBLE TRACKAGE SYSTEM

Please tell your friends about the Railway Modeller

GIANT O lima

at beatties

We have shown you LIMA HO gauge. NOW come along to your local BEATTIES branch and see LIMA GIANT O gauge. Magnificently modelled in British outline, in big, big 'O' gauge which enables you to really see the fantastic detail. In 12v. D.C. 2-rail, which makes it ideal for garden layouts. These model trains are also so reasonably priced that, in some cases, they are no more expensive than other makes of HO gauge! Illustrated above is the fabulous No. 6534. L.M.S. 0-6-0 Fowler Class 4F Red loco and tender. Price £9.75.

beatties *EUROPE'S LEADING MODEL SHOPS*

Tri-ang goes big!

Other notable firms of the inter-war years include Leeds Model Co and Bonds o'Euston Road, but the next significant development in O gauge came, ironically, from the firm that took over Hornby in the mid 1960s: the Tri-ang Big Big Trains. A 'Hymek-alike' battery locomotive and Mk.II coaches with openable sliding doors added much play value, but the system was discontinued in 1972. However, around the same time (it is understood that Triang Hornby assisted in making the range possible), the Italian firm Lima released some UK out-line equipment as part of a large continental outline system. Examples such as the 4F and Class 33, together with a range of wagons, are still obtainable on the second-hand market these days, and have proved an entry-level way to O gauge for many decades. Intermittent batches of Lima models in O have been produced as recently as the early 1990s.

When its foundation was being mooted in the mid 1950s, the Gauge O Guild very nearly did not have much of a speciality to promote. The mainstream ready-to-run market was losing out to OO with rapidity, and the numbers of what we

Top
The Tri-ang Big Big Train 'Blue Flier' of 1967, a fair replica of a Class 35 Hymek diesel hydraulic. *Photo: Pat Hammond*

Above left
A full-page advertisement from Tri-ang/Rovex for the Big Big range, as printed in the RAILWAY MODELLER for July 1966.

Above right
By May 1970, the range of Peco Streamline trackwork included O gauge products.

Right
Lima enjoyed a brief foray into O gauge; this ad ran in the October 1975 RM.

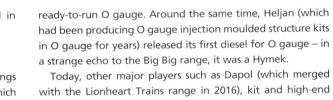

Above
The Bachmann Brassworks fleet of locomotives, produced ready-to-run in China, revitalised the fortunes of O gauge.

Right
The Danish manufacturer Heljan made its first move into O gauge locomotives with a Hymek.

would today call 'high net worth' enthusiasts who could afford the top-end creations of the likes of Beeson would not sustain the scale for ever.

Peco introduced its O gauge bullhead Streamline track in 1967, and pointwork a year later; flatbottom track was introduced in 1993, to cater for the increase in interest in more 'modern' period trackwork. Setrack plain track and points have also been released in recent years.

A 21st century rennaissance

Happily, over the succeeding 60+ years of the Guild, things have rebounded for O gauge, led chiefly by Bachmann, which launched its Brassworks range of locomotives and rolling stock in the mid-2000s. Other producers, and retailers such as Tower Models in Blackpool, have done much to popularise

ready-to-run O gauge. Around the same time, Heljan (which had been producing O gauge injection moulded structure kits in O gauge for years) released its first diesel for O gauge – in a strange echo to the Big Big range, it was a Hymek.

Today, other major players such as Dapol (which merged with the Lionheart Trains range in 2016), kit and high-end ready-to-run producers such as DJH, Lee Marsh Model Co and many others have ensured that O gauge has a very real future, as illustrious as its past century.

Right
Ready-to-run locomotives and rolling stock are today available from several sources. This GWR 64xx is in the Dapol range.

Chapter 2

Getting started in O

O gauge has existed since the very beginnings of the railway modelling hobby – pre-dating both OO and N – with popularity for the scale reaching its zenith during the first half of the 20th century when clockwork tinplate models from firms such as Hornby, Märklin and Bassett-Lowke were *de rigueur.* Having been surpassed by OO during the 1950s, and also N in more recent times, British O is now enjoying something of a revival following a wave of new proprietary models that have been produced in recent years.

Although at first glance the prices of O gauge products may appear expensive in comparison to their smaller-scale equivalents, it should be remembered that a small layout only requires limited trackwork, a couple of locomotives and a few items of rolling stock, and therefore the overall cost could be no more – if not less – than a more extensive N or OO gauge system occupying the same amount of space. Ultimately, a project in any scale will be as expensive as you decide to make it, and there is no reason why a satisfactory 7mm system cannot be achieved within the tightest of budgets.

Proprietary O gauge items

O gauge modellers are well served by the commercial model railway manufacturers, with an ever-growing array of ready-to-run locomotives, items of rolling stock, ready-to-lay track work and scenic accessories available off the shelf. Proprietary locomotives released in recent times also have provision for digital control and even digital sound. The following overview provides a flavour of what's currently on offer to would-be O gauge modellers:

An extensive range of locomotives and rolling stock is manufactured by Heljan, which has monopolised the diesel era market with the production of several diesel-electric and hydraulic classes including: 20, 26, 31, 35 (Hymek), 37, 40, 52 (Western), 55 (Deltic) and 60. Models of the AC Cars four-wheel railbus and BR Mk.I coaching stock has also been produced by the Danish company, together with several modern era wagons.

Ixion Model Railways has produced models of smaller prototypes of industrial parentage including a Manning Wardle 0-6-0ST and Fowler 0-4-0DM diesel mechanical shunter, both ideally suited to small shunting layouts.

In a similar vein, Minerva Model Railways has released a steady stream of models including a Peckett E class 0-4-0ST and 'Victory' class 0-6-0T.

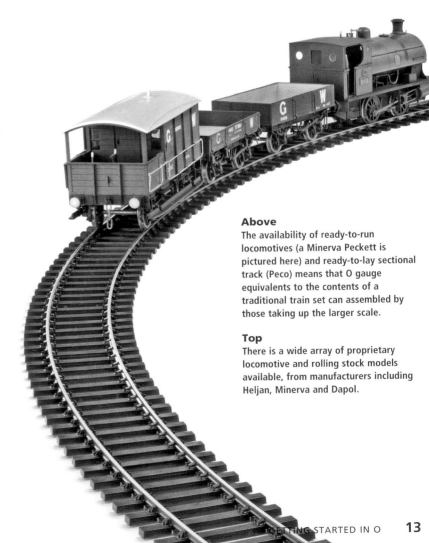

Above
The availability of ready-to-run locomotives (a Minerva Peckett is pictured here) and ready-to-lay sectional track (Peco) means that O gauge equivalents to the contents of a traditional train set can assembled by those taking up the larger scale.

Top
There is a wide array of proprietary locomotive and rolling stock models available, from manufacturers including Heljan, Minerva and Dapol.

Geared towards *aficionados* of the classic GWR branch line, Lionheart Trains has produced models of a 64xx 0-6-0PT, small Prairie, autocoach, B-set coaches and range of open wagons, all of which are now marketed under the Dapol umbrella.

Dapol's own releases include a Stroudley Terrier 0-6-0T, BR Class 08 diesel shunter, Fowler 3F 0-6-0T, GWR 57xx/'8750' 0-6-0PT, range of five- and seven-plank open wagons, various BR 10' wheelbase vans, six-wheel milk tanks, together with SR and BR pattern brake vans.

Ellis Clark, under the Darstaed label, has released extensive ranges of coaching stock models covering BR MK.I and BR suburban deisgns.

DJH offers a range of ready-to-run locomotives, which are effectively hand-built from the manufacturer's own kits, whilst there are also numerous fully-finished hand-built brass models marketed by companies including Lee Marsh, Finescale Brass and Masterpiece Models.

Bachmann Europe Plc at one time produced a range of locomotives and items of rolling stock for the British O gauge market under its Brassworks label; all manufactured in China from brass and sold as unpainted ready-to-run items. Although discontinued, examples do become available on the second-hand market. R-T-R brass models have

also been produced under the Tower Brass and San Cheng labels; although these are no longer manufactured, some items can still be obtained from the Blackpool-based O gauge specialist, Tower Models, usually as hand-finished items based on customer's specifications.

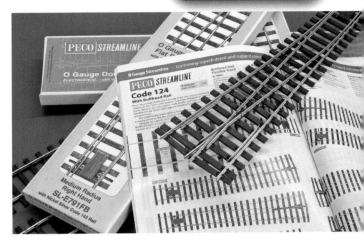

7mm scale support from kit suppliers

There are numerous suppliers of kits covering all manner of prototypes for locomotives, coaches and wagons; modellers depicting specific prototypes will find most of their needs can be met in kit form.

Largely of etched brass or whitemetal construction, most locomotive kits are best-suited to more experienced modellers, however, kits aimed at those with lesser experience are available from manufacturers such as DJH and Connoisseur Models. A plethora of coach kits is also available (arguably the poor relation in terms of current R-T-R availability), most of which are of etched construction, although a number of plastic kits are available from Slater's (which have etched components for some of the details) and other suppliers such as Ian Kirk and Roxey Mouldings.

Wagon kits are in plentiful supply, covering etched, white metal and plastic mediums. Extensive ranges of plastic moulded kits (many with etched components) are produced by suppliers including Parkside Models (by Peco), and Slater's.

Details of kit suppliers are published by the Gauge O Guild (see panel) in its quarterly Gazette publication, whilst the advertising pages of RAILWAY MODELLER include listings for many 7mm suppliers and is a good place to start for modellers seeking a model of a particular prototype.

Proprietary track

Ready to lay O gauge track systems are available from Peco – both sectional and flexible. The latter comprises both bullhead and flatbottom items. Peco also supplies a range of Individulay components to assist modellers with creating their own bespoke items of trackwork. These ranges are described in greater detail in chapter 6.

For further variety and specific trackwork needs, an extensive range of components for 7mm bespoke track construction is marketed by C&L Finescale, covering 'Fine', 'O-MF' and Scale Seven track standards. A custom-build service for bespoke trackwork is also offered by Marcway.

Scenic accessories

Whilst there are a number of 7mm scale kits available for lineside, industrial and domestic structures, this aspect of layout construction remains largely reliant upon scratch-building. To assist modellers there are numerous parts and components available from suppliers including Peco and Slater's Plastikard – the latter also producing embossed styrene sheet for brick, stone and wood surfaces. Whilst card kits are popular in OO and N, there are far less equivalent items available for 7mm.

There are, however, many ready-to-plant resin structures available from Skytrex Model Railways, together with a number of items produced by Bachmann Scenecraft.

One area where O gauge modellers are particularly well-served is with road vehicles, 1:43 being a long-established scale for die-cast cars, buses and lorries.

Ready-painted figures are produced by Preiser, albeit intended for the European market and with items manufactured to 1:43 and 1:45 scales (see page 18 for an explanation of the different scales adopted for O around the world). However, the scale discrepency is negligible and 1:45 scale figures would look perfectly acceptable on a British O gauge layout. For specific British-outline figures (such as railwaymen) then there are numerous cottage-industry suppliers including Dart Castings, Scale Link and Aiden Campbell.

Below
Most proprietary models have provision for DCC decoder installation. This Ixion Hudswell Clarke 0-6-0ST has an eight-pin socket and recess for a 20mm sound speaker.

Layout control

Many aspects of 7mm layout construction, such as layout wiring, can be treated in the same manner as for the smaller scales. However, analogue controllers are an area where O gauge differs, in that locomotive mechanisms (such as large Heljan diesel models) draw much more current than those in the smaller scales, thus requiring equipment with a higher output; suitable controllers with a higher current are available from suppliers including Gaugemaster.

Furthermore, the higher current draw of some O gauge motors necessitates the use of DCC decoders rated for a higher amperage. A power booster may also be required to ensure the 16v AC supply to the track can be maintained, particularly if multiple locomotives are in use simultaneously.

Layout control options and DCC decoder installation is covered in greater detail in chapter 6.

Model railway retailers

Newcomers to the hobby will find that the UK boasts a rich network of independent model railway retailers, many of whom have served the hobby for many years and are owned or staffed by people with much knowledge and experience. A visit to a local model shop – many of which carry stocks of O gauge items – is an ideal way to see first-hand what is currently available and also to seek advice for getting started with your own project.

A visit to a local model shop will also provide an opportunity to examine DCC control equipment first-hand, and allow you to judge for yourself whether locomotives fitted with light and sound functions are features that you

would like to have on your own model railway.

Naturally, in this day and age, purchasing model railway items can also be achieved at the click of a button, with many retailers having online shopping facilities with delivery to your front door.

Clubs and exhibitions

The country also has a large network of model railway clubs and societies, which offer a means of acquiring practical skills, sharing knowledge and seeking advice from fellow individuals in the hobby. Railway modelling can be a rather solitary pastime, so joining a local club has added social benefits too. There are, in fact, a number of clubs located around the UK that specialise in O gauge modelling – such as the Cornwall O Gauge Group.

The Gauge O Guild is the official organisation in the UK that represents and promotes the interests of O gauge railway modelling. There are various benefits to becoming a member, including newsletters and access to technical references.

A cursory glance at the event listings in a current issue of RAILWAY MODELLER magazine will reveal numerous exhibitions taking place at locations across the UK. Events take place every weekend throughout the year and range from

Below left
Local model shops can offer expert guidance with choosing the right items for your model railway project.

Below
Visiting model railway exhibitions provides opportunities to see O gauge products being demonstrated first-hand, including DCC sound systems.

Right
A feature of many shows are modelling demonstrations, such as here with 7mm etched rolling stock kit construction.

Far right
There is arguably no better source of inspiration for a layout project than visiting one of the many model railway exhibitions that take place across the UK throughout the year. This is *Grindley Brook* (built by Hillingdon Railway Modellers) in action at the 2017 Warley National Model Railway Exhibition.

Right
The permanent O gauge system built and maintained by members of Gainsborough Model Railway Society is open to the public on selected days.

Below
Ipford, one of the exhibits at Pecorama, depicts a classic Great Western branch line terminus. The 64xx 0-6-0PT and auto-trailer are ready-to-run models manufactured by Lionheart Trains (subsequently re-released under the Dapol label).

large shows such as the Warley National Model Railway exhibition in Birmingham, through to many smaller provincial shows at towns and villages, often held in leisure centres, schools and church halls. These events bring together many layouts and models that are the work of both clubs and individuals, which will provide plenty of ideas and inspiration for your own project, whilst also affording the opportunity to glean tips and advice from the builders and operators of the layouts on display.

There are several events that take place through the year that are dedicated to O gauge, such as Guildex (organised by the Gauge O Guild).

There are a number of permanent model railway exhibitions around the UK, including here at Pecorama, where a number of O gauge exhibits are represented amongst the layouts in action (including *Talpidae Plaster Castings*, which is described in chapter 9).

There is also the extensive permanent system maintained and operated by members of the Gainsborough Model Railway Society, which covers 2,500sq ft and is believed to be one of the largest O gauge model railways in the country. Depicting the East Coast Main Line from Kings Cross to Leeds Central, there are occasional public open days, details of which can be found via the society's website:
www.gainsboroughmodelrailway.co.uk

Getting started in O – a question of scale

Historically, O gauge referred to a track gauge of 1¼" (or 32mm) but is now almost universally taken to mean models built to a scale of 7mm: 1ft or 1:43.5. American O Scale, on the other hand, is 1:48 scale, but still uses 32mm gauge track. European O also adopts a scale of 1:43.5, but Swiss (and some German) outline models are to 1:45 scale – however, the scale difference between these is negligible and many modellers are content to use items from both.

Today there are three distinct British track and wheelset standards that have been adopted by modellers:

Coarse *standard originated from the old clockwork tinplate era and utilises coarse flanges and a deep rail section. Vast quanitities of proprietary equipment were produced over the years, with much still in existence.*

Fine *standard is the most common standard used by O gauge modellers today. The current ranges of ready-to-run models (from manufacturers including Heljan, Minerva and Dapol) conform to this standard, as does the proprietary track range manufactured for O gauge by Peco.*

Medium Fine *(O-MF) utilises the same wheel standards as*

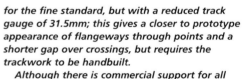

Left
German O gauge to 1:45 scale, modelled by Pete Martin.

Above
Canadian O gauge to 1:48 scale, modelled by Mike Dobson.

for the fine standard, but with a reduced track gauge of 31.5mm; this gives a closer to prototype appearance of flangeways through points and a shorter gap over crossings, but requires the trackwork to be handbuilt.

Although there is commercial support for all standards, the focus of this publication is on the 'Fine' standard, for which proprietary items are readily available. For anyone wishing to find out more about the other standards, referring to the Gauge O Guild website will provide ample information and advice:
www.gauge0guild.com

Finescale standards

For those who are interested in accurate scale standards, there is also Scale Seven, which broadly speaking is to 7mm scale what P4 is to 4mm. It uses tolerances developed from the prototype (including exact scale crossing dimensions) and a track gauge of 33mm. Wheelset and track standards are not compatible with the 32mm gauge standards and all trackwork needs to be scratchbuilt.

Proto48 serves a similar purpose for American modellers. Further information can be obtained by referring to the websites of the respective organisations:
www.scaleseven.org.uk
www.proto48.org

Right
Simon Thompson adopted Scale Seven standards for his extensive 7mm model based on Aberbeeg in South Wales.

Gauge O Guild

The Gauge O Guild has been serving the interests of modellers in this scale for over half a century. As well as standard gauge railways, the Guild also caters for those interested in the various narrow gauges modelled in 7mm scale. This nationwide organisation operates Local Area Groups, organises both local and national exhibitions.

Membership

Guild members receive copies of the *Gauge O Gazette*; published quarterly, this full-colour magazine usually runs to 96 pages and includes articles, product reviews and trade news. Members also have online access to all past issues of the *Gazette* (right back to the first newsletter published in 1956) complete with a searchable index. A sample issue of a recent *Gazette* can be downloaded from the website.

An informative newsheet accompanies each *Gazette* with news of members' and groups' activities and notice of forthcoming events. In addition the Guild's comprehensive technical manual is available to members, also now available online.

The Guild website contains a page with links to traders' websites as well as full contact details for each trader. There is also a product directory which members can use to find specific products, be it a complete kit or a small detailing part. Other online services provided by the Guild website include a club directory, news page, events diary and a members forum.

Guild shows

The Guild's flagship event is its annual convention, which in recent years has taken place at Telford. Alongside O gauge layouts and demonstrators, there is a bring and buy stand and support from numerous traders. The Telford convention also features an annual competition.

There is also a full calendar of dedicated O gauge events that take place around the country which are supported by the Guild; full details are published on its website.

Above
The Gauge O Guild Convention, held in September each year, is a good way for members to catch up on their layout projects. It's open to non-members at a higher admission charge – another reason to join! The mix of inspiring layouts and demonstrations is a great encouragement.

Chelagasa and Arigna inside and at Guildex

To find out more

The Guild's comprehensive website gives full details about the activities and history of the organisation, along with details for how to join online. For enquiries:

The Gauge O Guild
Tel: 0845 603 6213   email: gog@artytype.co.uk   www.gaugeOguild.com

Chapter 3

Inspirational layouts

B y the time that the infant RAILWAY MODELLER made its debut in late 1949, OO gauge was firmly entrenched in the minds of railway enthusiasts. Hornby Dublo was 11 years old, and other firms were picking up the pieces post-war. But whither O gauge?

The early editions of the magazine were dominated by in the main large systems such as *The Irish International Railway and Tramway System* by Cyril Fry, and *The Sherwood Section of the LMS* by Norman Eagles and his 'gang' of modellers. The latter was actually begun in 1921, and whilst its method of propulsion – clockwork – was probably considered *passé* even when it made its first appearance in RM in January 1952, it was to continue to be a feature of the publication through many rebuildings into the 1970s. It stayed true to its over-riding principles: being a model of a railway, with its operational requirements uppermost, rather than any considerations of 'scale', or scenic treatment beyond that which was essential. The Frys' system, commenced in the 1930s, was also extensive (25' x 15'), and notable for being situated in the Irish Republic, when the development of O gauge after WW1 was centred on the world-famous Northampton premises of W J Bassett-Lowke.

Yet 'scale' modelling was taken seriously by such pioneers and leading lights of O gauge as John Anning, G P Keen and W S Norris, who in conjunction with Bernard Miller created the well-known layout with stations named Francisthwaite and Stroudley, and a mix of top-quality Midland and LBSCR models. Norris was instrumental in forging two-rail current collection, disposing of the third rail for appearance's sake.

O gauge outdoors

Given the size of the models it is no surprise that O gauge has been used out of doors very successfully for many years. Exponents such as Jack Ray with *Crewchester*, Geoff Bigmore with *Bigston*, and Don Neale have all been trailblazers, the last-named not least for the magnificent 12-arch viaduct that strode across his lawn. Cast in concrete, the double-track structure ran on a 45' radius curve, carrying the trains 2' above the grass. Civils work in O gauge has seldom looked more magnificent before or since.

Above
The *Sherwood Section* was developed and refined over many years, and regularly featured in RM.

Below
The final version of the *Kendal Branch* project in O gauge by David Jenkinson, seen here with a Claughton departing the terminus.
Photo: David Jenkinson

Left
Nottingham Castle station was the operational hub of the *Sherwood Section*. A Hughes 4-6-4T has just arrived with a passenger service from Trent Town.
Photo: Philip J Kelley

Above
Geoff Bigmore developed his Great Northern-inspired *Bigston* with termini in sheds.
Photo: Cyril Freezer

Top right
Don Neale's centrepiece of his long-established garden railway was this 12-arch viaduct.
Photo: Don Neale

Right
Bromford and High Peak, a model railway without compromise.
Photo: Brian Monaghan

Into the 1980s

Celebrated layouts of the 1980s were rightly kicked off by one of the finest examples of money-no-object modelling in the form of *Bromford & High Peak*, which appeared anonymously in RM December 1979. It was owned by Colonel R J Hoare, and featured locomotives by such luminaries as Stanley Beeson and Vic Green – a truly remarkable feat of modelling skill. There was the series of projects by Ken Payne, and by the time the decade came to us David Jenkinson had abandoned his *Little Long Drag* for 7mm scale in the same space: various house moves saw iterations of his Kendal branch project come and go – and he also had time for Gauge 1 outdoors!

Yet arguably the most significant O gauge layout of the time was the one that starred in the never-to-be-repeated show at the Central Hall, Westminster, organised by *Model Railway Journal* magazine. This was *Hursley*, a Southern terminus by Martyn Welch, and it appeared in the November 1990 issue. Its publicity propelled the event to the dizzying heights of queues around the block!

This was followed a few years later with the Yeovil Model Railway Group's *Gas Works* project, a compact yet highly convincing depiction of a gritty industrial vista. Following its appearance in the April 1997 issue it was awarded that year's RM Cup.

Other notable layouts which have appeared in RM over the time have been the operations-based Eastern Region *Wallsea* by Barrie Walls and the Highland terminus *Laxford Bridge* by Dave Walker, who also took on the Irish scene with *Killaney*, which turns the wheel full circle.

In recent times

It would not be fair to single out layouts from the many that have graced our pages since the turn of 21st century: all readers will have their favourites, their inspirations to tackle O gauge themselves. However, in the following pages we present a few examples that cover a cross-section of O gauge modelling, from pre-Nationalisation steam through to the BR blue era, and compact micro end-to-end schemes through to expansive main line models with continuous runs. Something, we hope, to whet the appetites of everyone, whatever your personal modelling aspirations...

Below
Star of the one-off event at the Westminster Central Hall in London in 1990 was *Hursley* by Martyn Welch, a well-observed Southern Region terminus.
Photo: Martyn Welch

Right
Members of the Yeovil Model Railway Group created *Gas Works*, to exploit the space-saving capabilities of industrial O gauge locomotives.
Photo: Len Weal

Far right
Dave Walker's evocative Highland Railway terminus *Laxford Bridge* occupied a space of only 12' x 3'.
Photo: Brian Monaghan

The Tar Works

Created by Mike Perry

From RM December 2013

Proving that anyone can find the space to build a layout in 7mm scale, this exhibitable micro layout features a scenic section measuring just 4' long. A single point shunting piece with three sidings such as this may not be everyone's cup of tea, but it does offer an ideal way of getting a feel for the larger scale before embarking on something more ambitious. Small layouts can nonetheless be finely detailed, and be completed more easily than a larger layout might prove to be. Indeed, Mike noted in his RAILWAY MODELLER article that "The Tar Works came about in a rather haphazard way, which may inspire readers who are having difficulty starting, or finishing a large layout!"

Compact shunting layouts are also well-suited to 7mm scale, where the weight of the locomotives and stock aid slow running and make for satisfying operation. It represents a relatively inexpensive financial outlay too; just a handful of wagons, one small shunting locomotive and a single point being the key items for expenditure.

Mike describes how this micro layout has "provided hours of pleasure, not to mention teaching me a lot! It is lightweight, can be set up by one person, and is easily moved and stored."

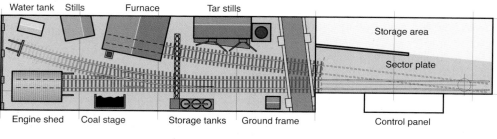

Water tank · Stills · Furnace · Tar stills · Storage area · Sector plate · Engine shed · Coal stage · Storage tanks · Ground frame · Control panel

THE TAR WORKS
Scenic area 4ft x 1ft 3in (overall length 6ft 3in). Each grid square = 1sq ft.

Victoria Park

Created by Ian Futers

From RM December 2008

This is one of a large portfolio of layouts, such as diesel depots and dockside stations, constructed by Ian that demonstrates just what can be achieved with limited trackwork in a small space. Although this compact urban terminus utilises just three points and occupies a scenic area of just 8' x 1'6", it still manages to offer plenty of operational interest. The layout illustrates what can be considered to be the smallest practicable concept that can be operated using main line locomotives in 7mm: in this case a stud of BR Type 2s, together with single and two-car DMUs. However, the track plan is also equally suited to a steam era model. This sort of layout also makes for a good interim project, or a diversion into a new timeframe.

Set in the Glasgow suburbs, Victoria Park represents the 1970s, when short-wheelbase rolling stock was still the norm – vital for a very small layout where every inch of space saved is of the utmost importance. It was inspired by Helensburgh, on the north bank of the River Clyde – but of course with a selection of different stock can be placed almost anywhere.

Ian explains how "such a project does not need a great deal of room and you can certainly work the layout with only a few chosen pieces of rolling stock, so it need not be expensive."

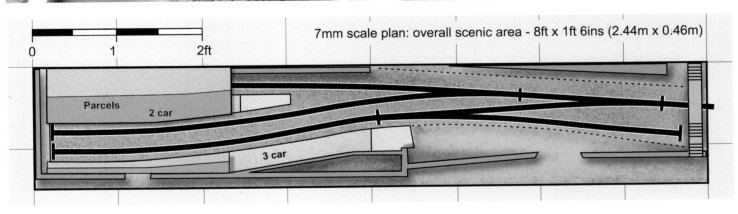

7mm scale plan: overall scenic area - 8ft x 1ft 6ins (2.44m x 0.46m)

0   1   2ft

Parcels   2 car   3 car

Clowne South

Created by James Harrison

From the 2015 RAILWAY MODELLER Annual

This small Traction Maintenance Depot is an ideal way of displaying a collection of diesel locomotives; this particular scene represents part of a larger depot, and is situated on a shelf in James's spare room. It was designed to be easily dismantled: as James noted "the problem was that I only rent a small flat, so I did not want to go building complicated baseboards, drilling holes in the wall or disturbing my neighbours by cutting up wood in the street."

The solution he chose was to utilise units from a well-known Swedish retailer, augmented by the chance recovery of some chipboard which had been used as protection for a pallet load. O gauge diesels are heavy, so a strong baseboard is a must. Although the shelf units are quite low, the layout is operated from the seated position using an office chair.

The locomotives themselves are all from the Heljan range and have been detailed and weathered to match photographs of specific machines. Some have been obtained as non-runners from swapmeets and the like; they are propelled and hauled by working locomotives as required, to suggest the repositioning of a failed or withdrawn locomotive.

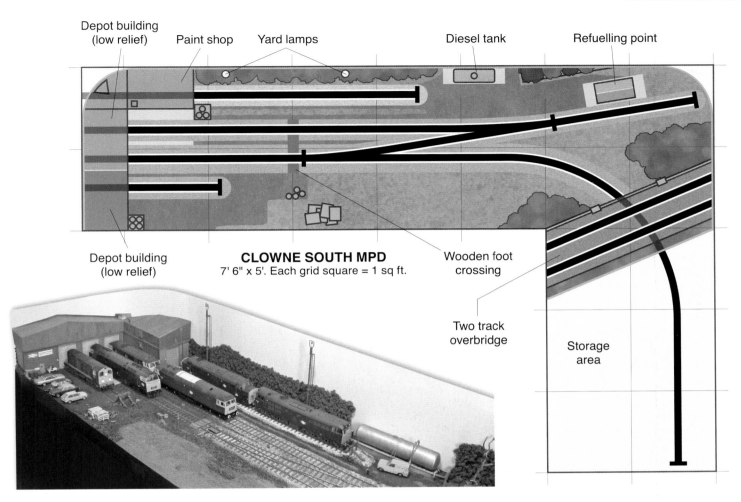

Depot building (low relief)
Paint shop
Yard lamps
Diesel tank
Refuelling point

CLOWNE SOUTH MPD
7' 6" x 5'. Each grid square = 1 sq ft.

Depot building (low relief)

Wooden foot crossing

Two track overbridge

Storage area

Plaxtol Road

Created by Tim Tincknell

From RM March 2015

Set during the 1930s, this branch terminus to fiddle yard model took its inspiration from the proposed – but never built – Hadlow Light Railway in Kent. The proposal for the HLR was made following the passing of the Light Railways Act in 1896, which was introduced to reduce the cost of railway construction and operation. Limits were imposed on the speed and weight of trains – typically to 25mph and 8T axle load – which allowed the use of lightly laid track and modest infrastructure. Many such lines were run with no signalling as a one engine in steam operation. The most prolific light railway engineer was Colonel H F Stephens.

The scenic section measures 8' x 2', fed by a two-road sector plate fiddle yard which brings the overall layout length up to 10'6". Trackwork was handbuilt in situ using code 100 flat bottom rail spiked with Peco track pins to scale 9' long sleepers of 1/16" ply. However the platform road utilises code 124 bullhead rail on 8'6" long sleepers, to create a contrast between the sidings and the main running line.

Locomotives and rolling stock are largely from Roxey Mouldings kits, with wagons from a variety of kits. The eclectic mix of items reflects the varied stock (which was often acquired second-hand) that a frequently cash-strapped real railway would have.

All stock is fitted with Dingham auto couplers, operated using electromagnets sited around the layout, energised by push buttons.

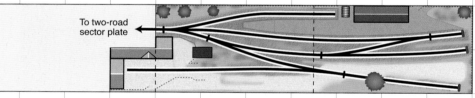

To two-road sector plate

Plaxtol Road
Overall layout size 10' 6" x 2'. Size of scenic section 8' x 2'.
Each grid square = 1 sq ft.

Bury Thorn Tar Works

Created by Dave Hall

From RM December 2014

This purely industrial layout represents a tar distillers and chemical works, set somewhere in the West Riding of Yorkshire. It is set during the early to mid 1960s. Tar distillers existed before the days of offshore natural gas to utilise by-products from the production of gas (for domestic and industrial use), every sizeable settlement having its own gasworks. Tar was sold to firms which distilled it into useful chemicals such as creosote, carbolic acid and pitch.

The reason for modelling a relatively obscure industry was to utilise vans and tank wagons; vehicles that look the same loaded as they do unloaded. Dave's aim was to capture the feel of a dirty industrial site with unkempt industrial engines.

Measuring 12'5" x 1'6", the layout is a permanent fixture in Dave's home, and has not been built for exhibition. However, the boards were constructed in three sections, which enables the layout to be moved easily if required in the future.

Trackwork is Peco bullhead throughout, with points operated using SEEP latching solenoids. The latching type is necessary because the over-centre springs have been removed from the points, together with the raised moulded ramps. The majority of the buildings were

scratchbuilt with a variety of materials used for the shells including styrene, plywood and foam board – all covered with embossed plasticard.

Locomotives and rolling stock are largely from kits, but a scheme similar to this could be created exclusively with ready-to-run items.

Bury, Thorn & Sons Ltd. Tar Works Overall layout size 12' 5" x 1' 6". Each grid square = 1 sq ft.

Frecclesham

Created by Newport MRS

From RM September 2014

Set during the BR steam era, the scenic section of this Southern Region branch terminus model occupies a scenic area of 14' x 3'. The station is served by a traverser fiddle yard (illustrated on p44) and the layout is equipped for DCC.

The track plan was devised using Templot software, with a key design goal being for the platform run-round loop to be of sufficient length to accommodate a three-coach train. The trackwork features a three-way point, single slip and double slip – these items saving 2" in length compared to creating the same formation with standard two-way points. The layout was inspired by the Westerham branch in Kent, and much of the rolling stock is to former South Eastern & Chatham Railway designs.

Trackwork was built by hand (using C&L components for the plain track), with the points and signals operated using MERG servo control boards.

Structures are all scratchbuilt, save for the signal box which is based on a Churchward Models etched kit. Trees were made using the twisted wire method, utilising products and kits from TreeMendous.

Unusually – but a method which paid off in the long run – the Newport MRS members responsible for the layout completed the presentational aspects of the exhibition layout – its fascia, complete with name board and so on – early on in the build, rather than rushing to finish this aspect in days before an exhibition commitment! Only when it was finished did the crew turn to tracklaying and scenery.

Frecclesham is operated from the front, enabling interested spectators to ask questions of the crew easily – when they're not busy shunting of course…

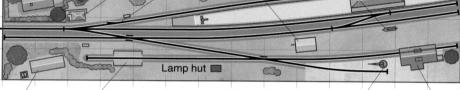

"Crun Rovin" holiday cottage   Signal box   Catch point   Water tower   Water crane   Station building

Lamp hut

"Minnies" barn   Base of derelict engine shed   Yard crane   Goods shed

FRECCLESHAM
14' x 3'. Each grid square = 1 sq ft.

Glen Nevis

Created by Chris Thorp

From RM January 2018

This homage to the West Highlands of Scotland in blue diesel days is housed in an attic space measuring 20' x 11'. The layout incorporates a terminus, through station, and continuous run on two levels. Inspired by the Fort William area, the track layout, buildings, scenery and timetable all borrow heavily from the prototype.

Peco track has been used throughout, with a minimum radius of 4'6". Point operation is a combination of manual and solenoids on those that are difficult to reach from the operating area. The layout is fully signalled by semaphores, constructed using signal parts from MSE; all are upper quadrant. They are operated by servos via a Megapoints control board.

The DCC controlled layout started out as a 12V dc project. Chris recalls that "the lure of DCC sound was too strong to resist!" The section switches – a legacy from the 12V dc operation – have been retained, however to assist with fault- and short-finding, should the need arise. The Roco Z21 system is used, operated on an iPad.

Three-link and screw couplings are used in the main, although Kadees are used for the intermediate couplings on fixed sets of coaching stock.

Lighting is a feature of the layout, produced using scratchbuilt posts from brass tubes and LEDs. Running trains in the dark is so atmospheric, making the layout a completely different experience.

"Glen Nevis is a wonderful reminder of the 1980s and my travels photographing Class 37s in the West Highlands."

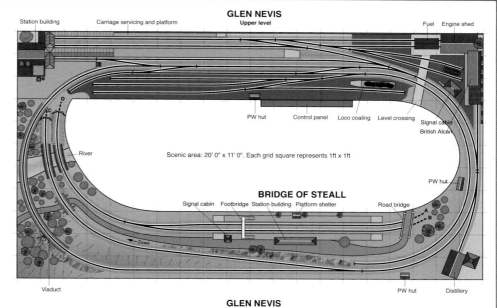

GLEN NEVIS
Upper level

Station building — Carriage servicing and platform — Fuel — Engine shed — PW hut — Control panel — Loco coaling — Level crossing — Signal cabin — British Alcan — River — Scenic area: 20' 0" x 11' 0". Each grid square represents 1ft x 1ft — PW hut

BRIDGE OF STEALL
Signal cabin — Footbridge — Station building — Platform shelter — Road bridge — Down — Viaduct — PW hut — Distillery

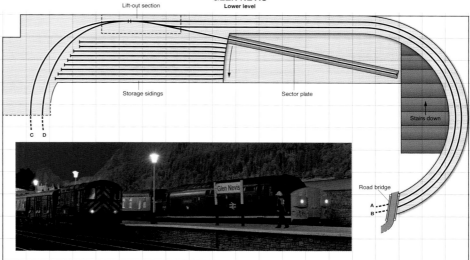

GLEN NEVIS
Lower level

Lift-out section — Storage sidings — Sector plate — Stairs down — Road bridge

Bucks Hill

Created by Kevin Wilson & Paul Bambrick

From RM January 2015

This magnum opus *celebrates the Great Western main line between South Wales and Hereford, specifically the section of line around Pontrilas, erstwhile junction for the Golden Valley branch line, complete with the distinctive short tunnel just south of the station.*

Constructed to exacting finescale standards, this digitally-controlled layout makes full use of the technology to feature sound and lighting effects, whilst the backscenes are the work of Paul's considerable talent in this area. The location was chosen because of its Great Western appeal; LMS running rights allowed crimson lake models to be run as well. The name was changed to allow trains not strictly true to the prototype to be operated.

Kevin and his friend Mike Morris constructed the baseboards; most of the hand-laid trackwork and some of the structures were the work of the late Carl Legg, another staunch supporter of this extensive project.

The layout has a full complement of scratchbuilt, working signals, matched to the prototype installation at Pontrilas, plus point rodding and other fine detail.

Despite its size, Bucks Hill is awash with tiny details, including custom-produced birds of prey from Aiden Campbell, and a detailed signal box interior – complete with notices and timetables etc – modelled by Peter Squibb.

Such a grand project is truly an inspiration!

BUCKS HILL

Scenic area: 48ft x 8ft   Each grid square = 1 sq ft

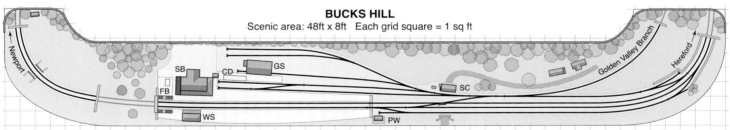

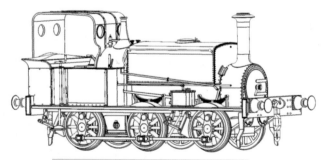

GAUGEMASTER COLLECTION

O SCALE LB&SCR TERRIER AND ROLLING STOCK

Pre-Production Sample

This limited run model - which is part of the Gaugemaster Collection - is sure to be a popular locomotive not only with 7mm modellers, but also with collectors and fans of the Southern Railway. Four versions are available to order.

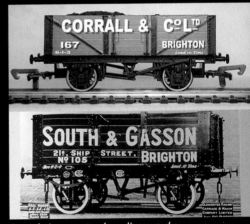

GM7210101 Terrier Brighton Works   RRP £229.95
GM7210102 Terrier Brighton Works (DCC-Sound)   RRP £449.95
GM7210103 Terrier Brighton Works Weathered   RRP £239.95
GM7210104 Terrier Brighton Works Weathered (DCC-Sound)   RRP £469.95

We are also producing two complementary Private Owner Wagons which will allow you to represent stock movements around the Brighton area.

GM7410101 5 Plank Wagon Corrall & Co Ltd Brighton   RRP £48.95
GM7410102 5 Plank Wagon Corrall & Co Ltd Brighton Weathered   RRP £49.95
GM7410201 7 Plank Wagon South & Gasson Brighton   RRP £48.95
GM7410202 7 Plank Wagon South & Gasson Brighton Weathered   RRP £49.95

Sample images to show livery only

BRIGHTON WORKS O SCALE PREMIUM STARTER SET - Available Autumn 2018

This starter set contains one Brighton Works Terrier Locomotive, one Corrall & Co Ltd Wagon, and one South & Gasson Wagon. The Peco O Scale Setrack included will allow you to build various end-to-end shunting layouts, powered by the Gaugemaster Combi controller included in the set. This is a fantastic way to start your O Scale layout, as it is easily expanded.

GM7000101 Brighton Works Premium Starter Set   RRP £429.95

GAUGEMASTER products are available from your local Model Shop or, in case of difficulty, direct from ourselves.

GAUGEMASTER Controls Ltd, Gaugemaster House, Ford Road, Arundel, West Sussex, BN18 0BN, United Kingdom
tel - 01903 884488 Fax - 01903 884377 email - sales@gaugemaster.co.uk web - **www.gaugemaster.com**

Chapter 4

Design considerations

Before embarking on the construction of your own O gauge model railway, there are some key issues that should be carefully considered and a suitable layout plan needs to be devised. As with any model railway – regardless of scale – these key issues are namely; modelling time available, your financial budget, finding a suitable location to house the layout, and establishing what you want to achieve with it. Making the right choices early on will pay dividends as the project progresses and will also ensure that, when complete, your model railway rewards you with countless hours of enjoyment and satisfaction.

As a word of caution, extensive main line systems with lengthy express trains are what many modellers aspire to build. However, such schemes often require a big financial investment to acquire sufficient locomotives and stock, not to mention the track and associated scenic items. Large layouts with lots of track and scenery also represent a big time commitment for construction too. Even if you do have the space available for such a grand plan, if this is your first foray into O gauge then a more modest scheme may prove to be the most sensible option.

Left
Eric Bottomley managed to squeeze a double-track continuous run into a space of just 17' x 17'. Named *Chadbury*, the layout is operated with a Lenz DCC system.

Right
Simon Thompson houses his *Aberbeeg* project in a purpose-built workshop, with the central area inside the circular layout used to house his classic car.

Below
Despite the scenic section of *Frecclesham* (by Newport MRS) measuring just 14' x 3', this rebuilt Bulleid light Pacific looks very much at home here.

Far right
Many exponents of the larger scales elect to use the greater spaces available with outdoor locations, such as Matthew Cousins' *Cadwell Moor*.

Below right
For those fortunate to have lots of space at their disposal, then grand schemes can be tackled – such as Pete Waterman's recreation of *Leamington Spa*, seen here in 2008.

Finding a home for your layout

Although, in comparison to 2mm and 4mm, everything is proportionally bigger in 7mm scale, one thing that doesn't change – regardless of scale – is the space available for housing a layout project. Therefore the key factor with O gauge modelling is the challenge of fitting a workable scheme within the available space – especially given the less than generous proportions of the average modern family home.

Home locations for a permanent or semi-permanent system that can be considered include a spare bedroom, attic, garage or garden shed. The larger scales are also well suited to an outdoor system, meaning that the garden also presents a viable option (see Chapter 12). A few examples are illustrated here to show what modellers have achieved in these varied locations.

The critical factor in O gauge is the minimum radius of

curves; Peco Setrack curves have a 40" radius, which means even a basic oval of track requires a board depth nearly 7' across. However, large locomotive models (such as express passenger classes) require an even greater operating radius of at least 48". Therefore, accommodating any kind of satisfactory continuous run in an average-sized family home is likely to be very difficult. As such, modest end-to-end systems naturally prove to be popular in 7mm, which also explains why there is a general lean towards branch line and industrial shunting layouts in this scale. Some spectacular main line and continuous run O gauge layouts have been achieved over the years (such as Pete Waterman's *Leamington Spa*), but these are the exception rather than the rule.

If you don't have room around the home for a permanent layout, then there may instead be room to store a portable set-up; one that can be kept out of sight when

not in use. Examples of such layouts are included throughout this publication.

Choosing a prototype and a theme

Once you have decided where your model railway is to be located (and consequently the maximum dimensions of your model), the next stage is to consider what you want your system to represent in terms of era and prototype. There are plenty of options and often what will appeal will be a result of your own memories of first-hand experiences of full size railways. Do you want to model steam or diesel outline – or even electric? Perhaps something based on a preservation centre or heritage railway? You may even wish to look further afield and model an overseas prototype of European, American or Japanese outline (see Chapter 13).

It is worth exploring the commercial availability of certain models at an early stage, as this may have a bearing on what era and prototype you ultimately choose to follow. As with OO, the most popular era with modellers is the BR steam/diesel transition period, encompassing the late 1950s through to the end of main line BR steam in

Above left
Dormston Terminus, Stephen Shepherd's portable branch terminus, has a scenic section just 7' long.

Above
Industrial themes are particularly popular in O gauge. This is *Bury Thorn Tar Works* by Dave Hall.

A representative selection of proprietary models available for different eras

Pre-Grouping	Pre-Nationalisation	BR steam	Pre-TOPS BR diesel	BR TOPS	BR Sectorisation	Post-Privatisation
Before 1923	1923 – 1948	1948 – 1968	Before 1973	From 1973	1983 – 1994	1994 onwards
S&DJR 0-6-0T (Dapol)	GWR '8750' 0-6-0PT (Minerva)	Stroudley Terrier (Dapol)	BTH Type 1 (Little Loco Co.)	BR Class 08 (Dapol)	Class 121 DMU (Bachmann Brass)	EWS Class 60 (Heljan)

Right
With small locos and short trains, light railways have long appealed to modellers. This model of the Selsey Tramway was built by Keith Smith.

Opposite left
Main line electric subjects are rare in 7mm; Graham Clark developed his own locomotive kit and scratchbuilt the overhead line equipment in the process of creating *Netherwood Sidings* – his tribute to the Woodhead Route.

Below
If rural scenic modelling doesn't appeal, then how about an urban dockside setting? This is *Worcester South Quay* by Alan Searle.

1968. However, pre-nationalisation, BR blue and privatisation eras – together with private industrial schemes – are also much in favour.

The scenic element of a layout is a major part of any layout project, although arguably less so in 7mm scale, where the available space often dictates that the scenic representation does not extend as far beyond the railway boundary as in the smaller scales. Nevertheless, the wider

setting for your railway should be carefully considered early on – do you want to model a rural outpost in the north of England with sweeping moorland scenery, or an urban metropolis with roads, buildings and industrial structures? To help with establishing a theme, many modellers compile lists of the key features they would like to include on their layout – such as goods yards, engine sheds, canals, industrial factories or quaysides. This list of essen-

Far left
Designing your own track plan requires nothing more than a pencil, ruler and graph paper.

Left
In contrast to the 'low tech' pencil and paper method, a more sophisticated approach is to use specialist track planning software, such as AnyRail as demonstrated here by David Malton. A free trial version of this programme is available to download from the internet.

tial criteria can then be used to assist with producing a suitable track plan.

Creating a track plan

For many, devising a track plan is a hugely enjoyable part of the design process. For the absolute beginner, it is probably most sensible to choose from published plans (a selection is included in this book) or you can create your own, perhaps by tailoring an existing plan that suits your aspirations and needs.

If you wish to create your own plan then you can use nothing more then a pencil and paper, but track planning computer software is also available, such as AnyRail, XtrackCad and WinRail. For either method, it is useful to have a few key measurements established before you start, such as the length of the longest locomotive you intend to use and the maximum train length. The accompanying table (Fig.1) provides some useful working dimensions to assist those drawing their own O gauge track plan.

Modellers moving up (from, say, 4mm scale) can use plans from the smaller scale as a source of inspiration for a 7mm project, although it is not necessarily just a case of enlarging one by 175%. Broadly speaking, a satisfactory-looking train in 7mm can be achieved with fewer vehicles than in 4mm, thus enabling platforms and run round loops to be reduced in length and sidings shortened, all helping to minimise the plan's overall length. Restricting loco lengths to smaller types (such as 0-4-0Ts) is also an effective way of maximising the space available if space for a layout is severely limited.

The greater space that O gauge trackwork requires is clearly demonstrated with the simple crossover illustrated here; using a pair of Peco medium radius points this will measure out at nearly 33" in length, so a run round loop sufficient for two Mk.Is – together with a headshunt long

Below
A useful aid for layout planning is the Peco range of downloadable track templates, which can be printed off to establish if a track plan is viable before purchasing turnouts and other track items. Illustrated here is an O gauge crossover, with a OO gauge one in the background for comparison.

Fig.1 Suggested minimum planning dimensions – inches (mm)

For standard gauge railways

Scale/Gauge	O
Point length (medium radius)	**16** (406)
Crossover (long)	**34** (864)
Minimum track centres	**3¹/8** (79)
Minimum radius curves	**48** (1220)
Minimum platform width	**4³/4** (120)
Min. overhead clearance	**6** (152)
Average coach (64')	**18** (457)
Typical wagon (10' wb.)	**6¹/4** (158)

Minimum length of loco release = length of loco over buffers + 10%

Suggested minimum length of headshunt = longest loco + three longest wagons

Note: These dimensions are nominal and meant as a guide for use when sketching out ideas. Always check out your plans with trials using paper point templates.

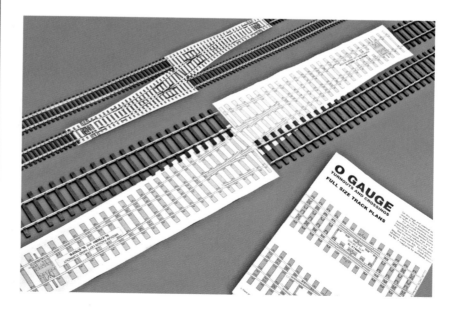

Above
Whilst plans may appear viable on paper (or even on screen), it is still prudent to undertake some practical checks using items of rolling stock and Peco paper track planning templates.

enough for a large tank engine – will equate to the best part of 8' in total; that's an awful lot of space to accommodate a very modest branch line consist!

Therefore, when it comes to devising a compact layout scheme, some degree of ingenuity and compromise is essential. There are ways of saving space, such as with the scenario described here by moving the crossover at the railway end of the loop 'off-scene', enabling its function to be substituted with a space-saving sector plate. This reduces the overall length required considerably, especially if the sector plate is utilised to form part of the set up for the fiddle yard and access to off-scene stock storage. Another option is to dispense with a run-round loop entirely and operate the model using a second loco to shunt the stock accordingly thereby releasing the train engine (see *Victoria Park* by Ian Futers for an example of this arrangement – as shown on p23).

Before investing in points and track, it is worthwhile proving a layout concept by undertaking some practical

checks using printed point templates (Peco point templates are available to download via the manufacturer's website) and a few items of stock that you may have available. This is the best way to check that your plan has adequate clearances on crossovers, that headshunts are long enough and that sidings can accommodate the intended number of vehicles.

Fiddle yard options

Most layout schemes will require an off-scene train storage facility of some kind. Having the capability to store multiple trains on the layout reduces the frequency with which models will need to be handled; this is a particular advantage with O gauge stock because the models tend to be much heavier.

There are various configurations of fiddle yard that can be adopted: For end-to-end schemes a traverser or sector plate arrangement is most commonly used (Figs.2 & 3). Turntable arrangements have been used for O gauge lay-

Fig.2 Fiddle yard sector plate

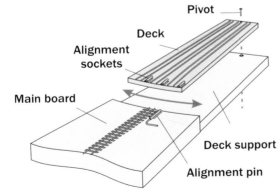

Right
Wood Street, a compact industrial scheme built by members of Swindon MRC, utilises a two-road sector plate that moves between the scenic section and a hidden storage siding that runs along the back of the layout. The sector plate also features a loco-release traverser.

Fig.3 Fiddle yard traverser

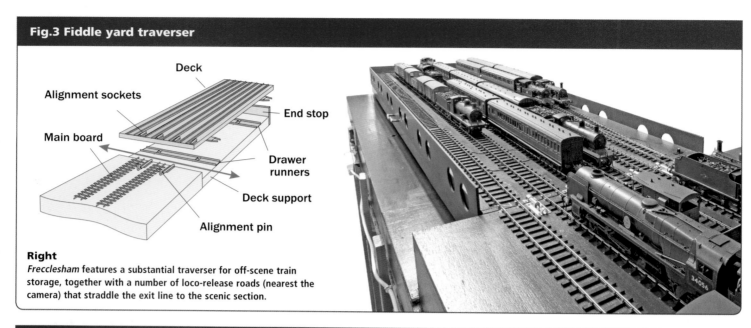

Deck

Alignment sockets

End stop

Main board

Drawer runners

Deck support

Alignment pin

Right
Frecclesham features a substantial traverser for off-scene train storage, together with a number of loco-release roads (nearest the camera) that straddle the exit line to the scenic section.

Fig.4 Cassette storage

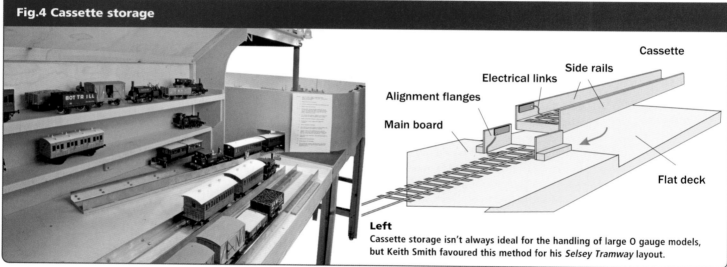

Cassette

Side rails

Electrical links

Alignment flanges

Main board

Flat deck

Left
Cassette storage isn't always ideal for the handling of large O gauge models, but Keith Smith favoured this method for his *Selsey Tramway* layout.

outs, but the greater overall length of trains in this scale, together with the greater weight of the models, means that they are not usually regarded as the most practical option. For similar reasons, storage cassettes are not as popular in the larger scale (Fig.4), but Keith Smith's *Selsey Tramway* layout is one example.

Baseboard considerations

Generally speaking, baseboard design and construction is little different for O gauge than it is for the smaller modelling scales, and traditional solid top or open frame timber types can be used. However, the construction – particularly of the trackbed supports on open frame types – needs

to be robust enough to support the heavier weight of many O gauge models. Consequently, this may translate into baseboards that are heavier per square foot than those built for a OO or N gauge set up – an important consideration if your layout is intended to be a portable system.

Lightweight methods of baseboard construction have been achieved successfully in O gauge, however, such as the use of extruded polystyrene and thin plywood described in the accompanying panel.

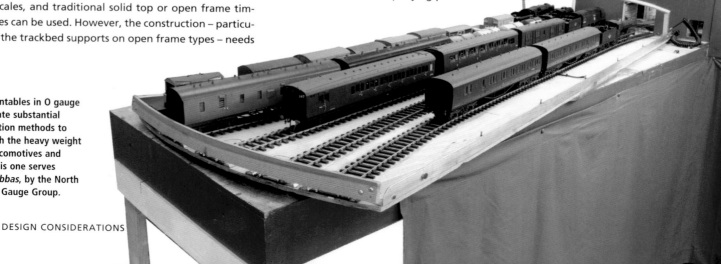

Right
Train turntables in O gauge necessitate substantial construction methods to cope with the heavy weight of the locomotives and stock. This one serves *Milton Abbas*, by the North Devon O Gauge Group.

Right
Michael Watts employed solid-top baseboard construction and proscenium arch style of presentation for his portable layout, *Webb's Wharf*, which is pictured here with Trevor Collins at the controls.
Photo: Adrian Colenutt

Below
The layout is supported on a pair of support frames to set the track height at 4'6" above the floor.

Below right
A view of the main layout baseboard under construction, showing the sub-structure supports for the raised areas of scenery.

BUILDING A LIGHTWEIGHT BASEBOARD

Gordon Gravett used a combination of extruded polystyrene and thin plywood to construct the baseboards for his compact Arun Quay layout. He used polystyrene for all the structural members (in place of traditional 2" x 1" timber), cladding these in 1/16" ply on all sides to make box sections that are extremely rigid yet lightweight. The outer faces of the completed boards were aslo clad in 1/16" ply, and the only use of thicker ply was where there was an interface between adjoining baseboards.

The downside to using extruded polystyrene is that the material is too soft to accept any screws or fixings. Therefore, Gordon cut rebates into the polystyrene to accommodate a ply insert to which point motors and uncoupling solenoids could be attached.

A strong all-purpose DIY adhesive was used to glue the polystyrene to itself or to timber, but a hot glue gun could also be used.

An example of Gordon Gravett's box section construction for the structural members (left), together with the underside of a completed board (right) and timber mounting point (inset).

Couplings

In contrast to the *de facto* tension locks fitted to ready-to-run OO stock, proprietary O gauge models are usually equipped with three-link or screw couplings, which enable items to be coupled together just like the prototype. An uncoupling tool, in the form of a simple bar with hooked end, is required for operation. However, some modellers may find three link couplings fiddly to use, in which case a method of remote uncoupling could be considered. Examples of the different options available include the Sprat & Winkle, Dingham and Alex Jackson systems of auto-uncoupling; each of these use magnets placed strategically between the rails to separate the coupling hooks between adjoining items of stock.

If the three link or screw couplings are to be used, one consideration to bear in mind is the propensity for the buffer heads of adjoining items of stock to become locked together when vehicles are being propelled around sharp curves. This is most likely to occur with items of stock that have a large overhang between the outermost wheelsets and the buffer heads, where the buffer heads are of a

Fig. 5 Buffer locking

Although three-link and screw couplings are totally realistic in appearance, one downside is that buffer locking can occur when propelling long vehicles around sharp curves (as pictured), which causes them to derail.

small diameter, and/or with vehicles of long fixed chassis length.

Opportunities for buffer locking to occur can be prevented by increasing the minimum track radius to suit the stock you wish to run, or restricting the stock to suit the track radius.

Hence, it can be seen how the establishing of a theme for your layout project – and therefore the locomotive and rolling stock requirements – goes hand in hand with devising a workable track plan.

Returning to the aforementioned alternative option of employing a method of uncoupling instead, these systems don't rely on the buffer-heads being in contact when vehicles are being propelled. Therefore, opportunities for buffer-locking to occur are eliminated.

Further reading

In this chapter we have looked at some of the key design considerations that relate to embarking on an O gauge project. However, many aspects of layout design are common across all scales, and further practical guidance is available in our other publications including titles in the 'Shows You How' series and *Your Guide to Railway Modelling & Layout Construction* (see Further Reading list on p122).

Below
The majority of ready-to-run O gauge stock is supplied with three-link or screw couplings, often with sprung hooks. A simple coupling bar (inset) is all that is needed for operation.

Above
One option for the remote coupling/uncoupling of stock is the Alex Jackson system, which uses home-made fine wire hooks that are drawn downward by magnets to enable uncoupling to take place. Delay action uncoupling can also be performed.
Photo: Gordon Gravett

Above & right
Tim Tincknell employed Dingham auto couplers on his *Plaxtol Road* layout, which take the form of brass hooks and loops, operated with electro-magnets sited around the layout. The stock is handed, with loops fitted only at one end of vehicles.

Chapter 5

Layout electrics, train control and DCC

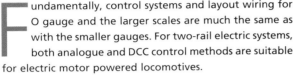

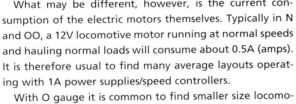

Fundamentally, control systems and layout wiring for O gauge and the larger scales are much the same as with the smaller gauges. For two-rail electric systems, both analogue and DCC control methods are suitable for electric motor powered locomotives.

What may be different, however, is the current consumption of the electric motors themselves. Typically in N and OO, a 12V locomotive motor running at normal speeds and hauling normal loads will consume about 0.5A (amps). It is therefore usual to find many average layouts operating with 1A power supplies/speed controllers.

With O gauge it is common to find smaller size locomotive motors running with similar current consumptions, examples such as the Minerva GWR 0-6-0PT, Heljan Class 05 and Dapol Terrier 0-6-0T operate with a maximum current draw not more than 1A. Therefore the same decoders can be used as those intended primarily for OO gauge models. Larger locomotives however, with physically larger motors, and some of the twin-motored diesel models in O, can require up to 2A just to get the loco moving. It can be a similar scenario in Gauge 1 and Gauge 3, where motors may be even bigger.

Although a small O gauge branch line or shunting yard layout utilising only small locos might well cope with a 1A power supply, if your ambitions are for a large layout with long trains and big engines, you will almost certainly require a beefier 5A supply, such as offered by controller manufacturers Gaugemaster, Helmsman and others.

DCC

It follows therefore that if some models in O gauge and larger, need more traction current, the application of DCC

Right
Integral transformers and speed controllers for O Gauge and larger. A 2.5A 12V dc Model PO from Gaugemaster, which includes brake and inertia simulation (top) and a 5A 12V dc unit from Helmsman.

Below
DCC decoders for O gauge. On the left are 8-pin and 21-pin examples from Gaugemaster, with a Soundtraxx ECO-400 4A decoder for O gauge diesels, on the right.

will require decoders of sufficient capacity to cope with the increased current, and likewise, a corresponding DCC system with a sufficiently powerful booster.

So, where to begin? Decoders and associated items for after-market installation are available from many different suppliers including Gaugemaster, Zimo and Soundtraxx. Some examples are illustrated below, and in the accompanying step-by-step sequences overleaf.

If you are buying ready-to-run O gauge locomotives, some manufacturers have already taken the guesswork out of identifying the decoder requirements. Minerva Models' locomotives include 8-pin sockets for standard

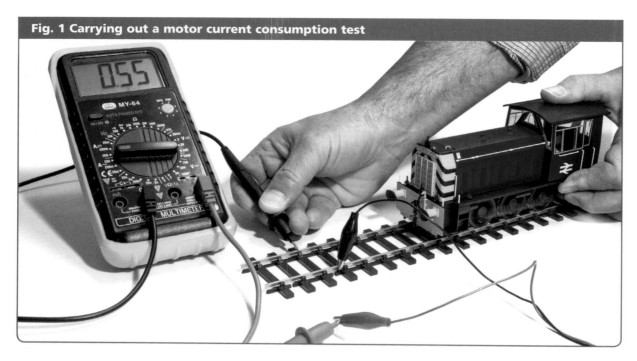

Fig. 1 Carrying out a motor current consumption test

control decoders for motor current to be plugged in. Dapol on the other hand, has engineered the total current requirements for motor, lights, sound, etc., at the design stage, to match the specified output parameters of industry standard 21-pin combined sound and control decoders. Accordingly Dapol's new models (at the time of writing in 2018) are supplied with factory-fitted 21-pin sockets, and in some cases factory-fitted speakers for sound effects.

This also allows the user to select a 21-pin decoder of his or her own choice, plug it into the on-board socket and set up the CVs straight away.

However, not all O gauge ready-to-run manufacturers have gone as far as to install decoder sockets of any sort, leaving the purchaser to hardwire the models for DCC use themselves. This is much the same situation for Gauge 1 ready-to-run locos too, and in consequence, fitting DCC to these models is in many ways similar to kitting out a kit- or scratchbuilt model.

Invariably locomotive kit producers might recommend any number of different motors, leaving the final choice to the builder. This inevitably produces a wide range of pos-

sible power requirements, especially if other ancillaries such as lighting, smoke units, operating fans, etc., have also been fitted to the model.

To determine the power consumption in these situations, so that a correct capacity decoder can be selected, a consumption test should be performed.

This consists of wiring an ammeter (a multimeter set to Amps is equivalent) between a DC controller and the model (*without a decoder fitted*) and measuring the normal running current and the stall current, as shown in Fig. 1. If you have a rolling road device, the test can be performed on that, otherwise on a length of track, grip the model in one hand and turn up the power letting the wheels spin freely. This will give a reading of the running current. The stall current can be measured by holding the loco firm against the rails, so that the wheels are held stationary against the torque of the motor – take extreme care with this and do not do it for more than a couple of seconds as damage to the motor or the gearing could result.

The stall current will likely be far beyond that which a decoder can provide, but any such extreme situation as this would normally be protected by the DCC system cut-out anyway.

The illustrated test in Fig. 1 shows a 0.55A running current measured using a multimeter.

If ancillaries are fitted, these should be tested individually for current draw and the total consumption calculated, however bear in mind that auxiliary function outputs on decoders are often lower rated then the motor outputs so you may be limited to the type of ancillary that can be fitted.

For example, smoke units inevitably draw more power than a motor (sometimes 2-3A) and may also include separately powered fans to produce the smoke effect. In these situations consideration should be given to powering the smoke

Left
This Large Prairie from Lee Marsh Model Co is supplied factory fitted with DCC, but can also run on 12V dc thanks to the convenient changeover switch located in the smokebox.

FITTING AN 8-PIN DECODER TO A MINERVA GWR/BR 8750 0-6-0PT

1

This model is equipped with an 8-pin socket inside the boiler cavity for fitting of a suitable decoder. Access to it requires removal of the locomotive body, achieved by unscrewing the four screws that hold the body and chassis together; there is a pair located at the front (pictured, inset) and another pair at the back.

2

3

There is a balancing pipe moulding that runs underneath the boiler barrel casting between the two pannier tanks. It is fitted in two halves and needs to be unclipped to enable the body and chassis to be separated.

With the body removed from the chassis, the mechanism is revealed together with the DCC decoder socket and blanking plug. The blanking plug needs to be removed carefully from the socket (inset). Avoid twisting or levering the plug out of the socket as this could damage the fine connecting pins.

4

A Gaugemaster 8-pin 4-function decoder was installed (ref.DCC29), making sure that the decoder was orientated correctly (pin No.1 on the decoder needs to be aligned with pin No.1 on the PCB socket). The decoder is rated for a maximum of 1.5A operating current, which makes it only suitable for smaller O gauge locomotive models. Once reassembled the decoder can be programmed in accordance with the manufacturer's instructions.

1

This model is equipped with a 21-pin socket for a combined sound and motor control decoder, should the user wish to fit a speaker and sound chip. However a 21-pin motor control only decoder can be fitted instead, as shown here. The socket is located inside the bonnet assembly. Access to it requires removal of both the bonnet and cab assemblies, achieved by first unscrewing four small screws underneath each corner of the cab (inset).

2 There are also two long bolts located at the front of the chassis (behind the front buffer beam) that need to be removed. The bonnet and cab assemblies can now be detached from the body. Note that there are wires for the cab-lighting that remain attached between the cab and chassis.

3

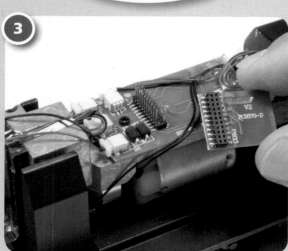

The DCC blanking plug can now be removed. Avoid twisting or levering the plug out of the socket as this could damage the fine connecting pins.

4 For this model a Gaugemaster 21-pin four-function decoder was used (ref.DCC27). It is rated for a maximum operating current of 1.8A. Prior to installing the decoder the model was tested to determine its running current, which was found to be 0.55A. Once reassembled the decoder can be programmed in accordance with the manufacturer's instructions. Note the circular cavity behind the front radiator to allow for fitting a speaker if the digital sound option is to be utilised.

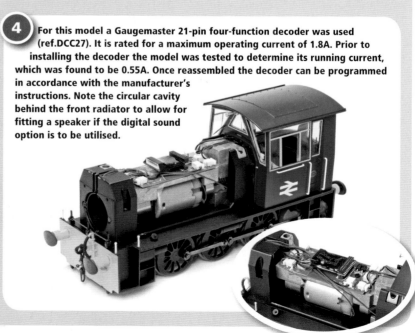

unit heater direct from the pickups, with the fan or 'blower' motor (to produce puffs of smoke synchronised with the sound) powered through a decoder controlled relay. It is perhaps fortunate that the larger bodies of O gauge models have sufficient space within for locating the myriad of components that such projects need.

Happily, for those modellers less technically minded, there are numerous firms offering DCC decoder fitting options for models that do not have factory fitted sockets. If you want to have go at fitting plug-in decoders yourself, two step-by-step examples appear on the previous pages.

Layout wiring

As mentioned above, whether your layout is to be analogue or digitally controlled, wiring elements such as track sections, polarity change-over on point, slip and diamond frogs, reversing loops, etc., is little different to that of the smaller scales. Some information on this topic can be

sourced in Chapter 6 Track Topics, but comprehensive layout wiring information is available in our PM-200 volume *Your Guide to Railway Modelling and Layout Construction* – see bibliography on page 122.

Battery power and live steam

If two-rail electrification and DCC options appear rather daunting, don't forget that the larger scales offer some interesting and fun ways of powering your locomotives by battery power or live steam.

Both these means can be used in conjunction with wireless radio control systems – ideal for garden lines with live steam (see chapter 11) – but also suitable for use indoors with battery locos, thus eliminating any need whatsoever for adding wires to the trackwork. There are a number of commercial suppliers offering R/C systems and the larger scale societies are usually able to offer further advice on this topic.

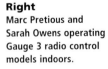

Track topics

This chapter introduces the options for trackwork available to modellers embarking on an O gauge project, including an overview of sectional and flexible track systems, together with track laying considerations and electrical wiring specific to this scale.

A summary of the Peco ranges of O gauge track are presented below – for full details refer to the manufacturer's product catalogue. It should also be noted that information relating to trackwork options for the larger scales of Gauges 1 and 3 are provided in Chapter 10.

Layout wiring is a very extensive subject in its own right and much of it is common to all scales. Accordingly, more general detailed information to help you with the electrical stage of building your model railway can be found in *Your Guide to Railway Modelling & Layout Construction*, together with several of the Peco 'Shows You How' pamphlets (see bibliography on page 122).

Sectional track

A recent innovation from Peco is Setrack items for O gauge, comprising straight units (length 168mm) and curved units (40½" radius, 16 per circle), together with right- and left-hand points, also of 40½" radius. Clip-together sectional track is perhaps more suited to beginners because it requires no cutting or pre-forming of curves. This also means that it can be assembled quickly – preferred by those who is eager to run trains!

Left
The Peco Setrack range for O is very easy to use and is ideal for beginners because no rail cutting is required.

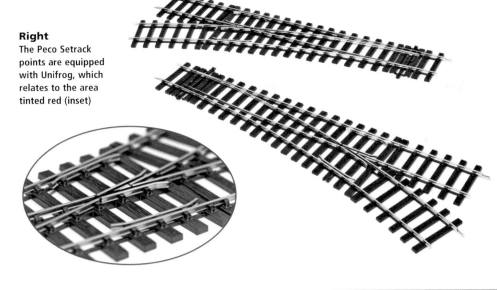

Right
The Peco Setrack points are equipped with Unifrog, which relates to the area tinted red (inset)

Above
The use of flexible plain track enables gentle sweeping curves to be created. These reverse curves were formed using code 124 bullhead track.

Sectional track can be laid for temporary 'table top' operation (like a train set) – the components being durable enough to withstand repeated connecting and dis-connecting. However, for a more permanent layout scheme, the track can be pinned or glued directly to a baseboard surface. PVA or impact adhesive can be used. The track can also be laid on a sub-base (from cork or balsa) if preferred, which helps to absorb the sound from locomotive mechanisms when operating the layout. This method is shown as part of the Setrack layout build that forms Chapter 9.

Setrack points are only available equipped with Unifrogs which means they can be used as supplied, with electrically insulated frogs, or, by adding an auxiliary switch, with the frogs electrically live (known as 'live' frog). For further details on this topic see under paragraph entitled Specific wiring considerations for O gauge trackwork, later in this chapter.

For any design of layout the minimum desirable radius will have to be determined. Generally, the larger the radius the better, but this is likely to be a compromise based on fitting everything into the available space. Peco Setrack is manufactured close to what is regarded as the minimum practical radius for O gauge of 40" and, whilst this is perfectly adequate for the majority of ready-to-run models that are available (particularly small steam locomotives, diesel shunters and four-wheel wagons), some larger models (such as large bogie diesel classes) may not operate satisfactorily around such tight curves.

The sectional track is fully compatible with the code 124 bullhead rail Streamline items (described below), so if in the future you decide to progress to the latter track type, the investment in Setrack will not be wasted.

Flexible track

In contrast to sectional track systems, flexible track does require the curves to be formed by hand and rails to be cut and joined. Essentially, flexible track allows for more versatile track formations which look even more realistic than that which sectional track offers. In particular, curves can be laid to more generous radii, whilst the more extensive range of points, slips and crossings that are available enables much more complex junctions to be assembled.

The cutting of plain flexible track to exact lengths does

Below
Eric Bottomley made extensive use of flexible track to create the entirely curved track formation on his layout, *Chadbury*.

Above
The rails of flexible plain track can be cut to length using a razor saw and a wooden block.

require a greater level of skill and dexterity than laying sectional track, however, if you are a newcomer to the hobby, the required techniques can be mastered quickly. There are also occasions when the sleeper ends of plain flexible track will need to be trimmed to join sections to the exit routes of points, as demonstrated in the accompanying panel.   It should also be noted that plain flexible track is only suited to setups where it can be pinned or glued down on a dedicated baseboard.

The Peco O gauge range of Streamline products includes items with code 124 bullhead rail and wooden sleepers; medium radius points (left- and right-hand), a medium radius Y point, curved points (left- and right-hand), long crossing, double slip, catch points and lengths of plain flexible track. The double-slip is the most complex item of trackwork currently available in the Peco O gauge range. Its use can save a lot of space compared to arranging a pair of two-way points 'toe to toe' (see Fig.1). It is therefore a popular item amongst modellers who are looking to maximise the space available for their layout.

Suited to layouts depicting main lines set in the late steam era onwards, some Code 143 Streamline flat-bottom rail items are also available, comprising medium radius points (left- and right-hand) together with yard lengths of plain flexible track. X

Note that at the time of writing (2018), all Peco

TRIMMING THE SLEEPER ENDS ON FLEXIBLE TRACK

1 This picture shows the conflict between sleeper ends that occurs when attching sections of plain flexible track to the exit routes of pointwork.

2 The solution is to trim the adjacent sleeper ends on each of the exit routes. For this example here, the first nine sleeper ends were trimmed as illustrated. A steel rule and a modelling knife was used to first mark a line across the surface of the sleepers, with a razor saw used to trim them as required.

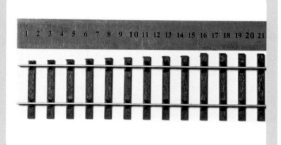

3 The resultant arrangement illustrates how trimming the sleeper ends has enabled an even and visually balanced sleeper spacing to be achieved.

Streamline points for both code 124 and 143 are equipped with Electrofrogs, for which the wiring considerations are described later in this chapter.

Flexible bullhead track can be joined using Peco nickel

Fig. 1 Illustration of the space-saving benefit of using a double slip

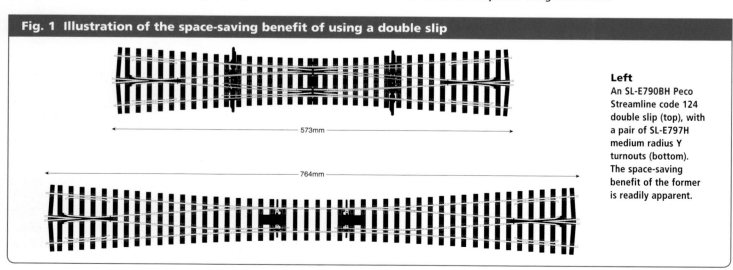

573mm

764mm

Left
An SL-E790BH Peco Streamline code 124 double slip (top), with a pair of SL-E797H medium radius Y turnouts (bottom). The space-saving benefit of the former is readily apparent.

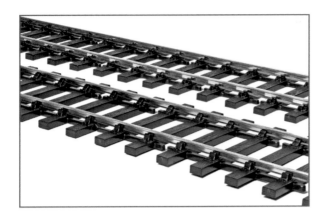

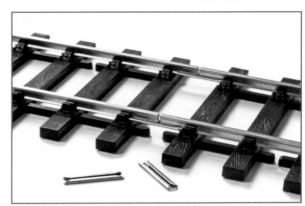

Left
A comparison of Peco Streamline flexible track; code 124 bullhead (front) and code 143 flatbottom (back).

Right
Peco SL-10 nickel silver rail joiners can be used to join code 124 bullhead track items.

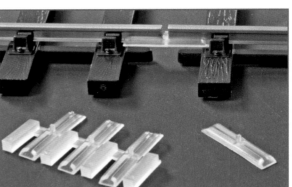

Left
The Peco transition track (SL-713) enables sections of bullhead and flatbottom track to be joined.

Right
For insulated joins on code 124 bullhead track, Peco SL-11 joiners can be used.

silver rail joiners (SL-10), with Peco SL-11 joiners used for insulated rail breaks. For flatbottom rail, SL-710FB nickel silver rail joiners and SL-711FB insulating rail joiners can be used. A useful item in the Peco range is the SL-713 transition track, which is intended for use between sections of code 124 bullhead and code 143 flatbottom track.

Below & Left
Concrete sleeper bases are available in the Peco Individulay range, to be used in conjunction with code 143 flatbottom rail.

Peco Individulay components
Peco also supplies a range of Individulay track components intended to aid modellers with the construction of their

Below
Tim Tincknell used a variety of items from the Peco Individulay range to build the trackwork on *Plaxtol Road*, which depicts a light railway.

own bespoke trackwork including; chairs, point blades and plain rail section.

Concrete sleeper sections are also produced, which can be used in conjunction with lengths of code 143 flatbottom rail to create concrete-sleepered track.

Other options
For bespoke items of trackwork not catered for in the Peco ranges, there are specialist suppliers that supply 7mm track components to assist modellers wishing to construct their own. These suppliers include C&L Finescale and Marcway; further details about their products can be sourced from their respective websites.

Specific wiring considerations for O gauge trackwork

Although general layout wiring topics are not covered here, there are aspects of wiring that are specific to O gauge trackwork, especially if using Peco track, including; how to add dropper wires, fit solenoid point motors, adding auxiliary switches to change the polarity of points in live frog mode, and the switching arrangement for the Streamline double-slip. It should be noted that the following practical guidance is equally relevant to analogue 12V dc or DCC control systems.

Attaching dropper wires to rails

Peco manufactures rail joiners with dropper wires pre-attached (PL-80) that are suitable for use with code 124 bullhead rail. An alternative method of connecting power to the track is to solder dropper wires directly to either; the rail joiners (on code 143 flatbottom track), the undersides of the rails prior to laying the track in place, or to the outside faces of the rails if the track has already been laid.

Methods of point operation

As supplied all Peco O gauge points are ready to lay and capable of being changed by hand by literally reaching across and pushing the point blades over with your index finger; in fact the moulded spigots on each end of the tiebar are fitted for that purpose. On a first layout, this method represents the simplest way to get started and there are many modellers who are quite content with this.

As skills develop it often becomes desirable to have the

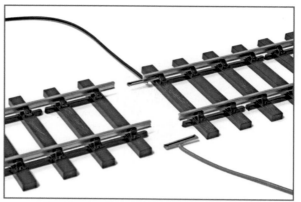

Left
A straightforward method of connecting power to code 124 bullhead track is to use Peco PL-80 rail joiners, which have wires pre-soldered to them.

points remotely operated, which helps to create a more realistic effect and allows points to be changed from a central control area, rather than having to reach across the layout – a problem perhaps, on large layouts and where

Left
Moving the point blades can be undertaken manually by hand, without the need to equip them for remote operation.

ATTACHING DROPPER WIRES DIRECTLY TO THE RAILS

1

This method is applicable to sectional or flexible track (bullhead or flatbottom). Turn the section of track upside down and cut the required sections of sleeper base away, as demonstrated, to allow wires to be soldered to the underside of each of the rails. Side cutters are ideal for this. Note how the locations are offset on each side so that the sleeper base is not completely severed. Code 143 flatbottom track is illustrated here.

2 The ends of the wire droppers and the exposed sections of rail are first tinned with solder. The wire is then soldered in place as shown, with care taken to avoid melting the plastic sleeper base with the tip of the iron.

3

The wire droppers fixed in place. Corresponding holes are drilled in the baseboard, or trackbed, to allow these to be passed through and connected to the main layout wiring loom/power bus (inset). Once the track is ballasted the wires are all but invisible.

Right
There are various means of moving the point blades remotely. One option is to use the Peco SmartSwitch servo system. These can be mounted on top the baseboard (as pictured), or below the baseboard.

points are located in hidden or difficult to reach areas.

To operate a point remotely, a suitable mechanism to slide the tiebar from side to side has to be fitted. This action can be achieved either mechanically using a 'wire in tube' method whereby an operating wire is linked to a handle or knob at the edge of the baseboard, or electrically using a solenoid motor, such as the Peco PL-10 or PL-10E, a slow acting point motor such as a Tortoise motor, or a servo as per the Peco 'SmartSwitch' control system.

The accompanying step-by-step sequence shows one of these remote point operation options; the Peco PL-10E solenoid motor mounted under the board directly beneath the tiebar.

INSTALLING A PECO PL-10E TWIN SOLENOID MOTOR FOR REMOTE ELECTRIC POINT OPERATION

1

To install a Peco solenoid motor underneath the baseboard the first task is to mark where to drill the hole through the board surface for the operating pin to pass through. The hole needs to be positioned with the tiebar 'mid-throw' so offcuts of thick card were inserted between the blades and the outer rails to hold the tiebar in the required position. A small drill bit in a pin vice was used to mark the position of the hole.

2

The hole was drilled out to 9.5mm. The photograph shows the point being laid in position and fixed in place in readiness for installing the motor.

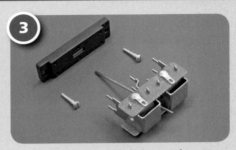

3

The PL-10E has an extended operating arm to allow for the depth of the baseboard. A plastic mounting plate (PL-9) is required to attach the motor to the underside of the baseboard.

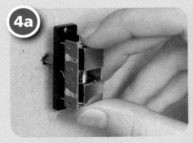

4a **4b** **4c**

Working from underneath the baseboard, the operating pin is passed through the baseboard and the tiebar of the point (a). Orientate the motor so that the sideways action of the operating pin is directly in line with the movement of the tiebar. Holding the motor in position, mark the two mounting holes for the bracket (b) and drill small pilot holes to accept the brass screws provided (c).

5

Remove the card pieces and check that the throw of the point is satisfactory by manually moving the operating pin by hand. If the blades fail to move all the way across then adjust the position of the motor to suit. Once satisfied that the point is throwing correctly, the excess section of the steel operating pin can be trimmed using a heavy duty set of side cutters.

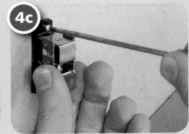

6

The Peco PL-34 wiring loom makes for straightforward connecting up of the point motor without the need for soldering.

7

A switch for controlling the operation of the point can take the form of a Peco passing contact switch (PL-26R/Y/B/W) mounted into a mimic diagram as part of a centralised layout control panel.

Unifrog and Electrofrog points

As mentioned previously, there are two types of frog fitted to Peco points, the Unifrog, as supplied with Setrack points, and the Electrofrog, as fitted to Streamline points. So what is the difference?

With the Unifrog arrangement, both routes out (downstream) of a point remain powered, regardless of which way the point blades are set. This is advantageous for DCC controlled layouts which require all track sections to be permanently 'live'. 12V dc analogue users, on the other hand, who wish to isolate one or both of the routes from the point, must fit insulated rail joiners (SL-11) between the point and the downstream sections of track. Separate power feeds, controlled via on/off switches mounted on a control panel are then required for these sections.

With the Electrofrog arrangement, only the route out of the point to which the blades are set is live, this means that the electrical polarity (+V or -V) of the frog changes dependent on the route set and as such, if power feeds are required downstream of the point (such as in a run round loop, or a plan with kick-back sidings) insulating rail joiners have to be fitted as close as possible to the two frog rails. The instructions included in the point packaging explain this fully.

Auxiliary frog switching

Peco Unifrog Setrack two-way points

Earlier in this chapter we noted how the Setrack points are equipped with Unifrog, which means they can be used in either insulated frog mode or live frog mode. The advantage of a powered frog is that it alleviates the need for locomotives to traverse an electrically 'dead' frog area, which could cause short-wheelbase locomotives (or models with limited electrical pick-ups) to hesitate or even stall completely, especially when running at slow speed.

To power the insulated frog tip and adjacent wing rails, a Peco PL-33 microswitch can be fitted into a PL-19 housing, which is then clipped onto the end of the Setrack point tiebar; with the microswitch wired according to the accompanying diagram (Fig.2), the movement of the tiebar triggers the microswitch, thus changing the polarity of

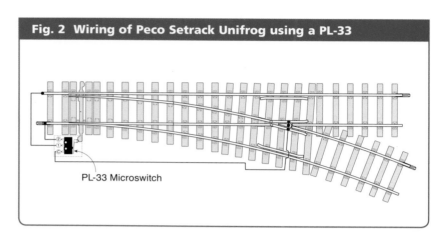

Fig. 2 Wiring of Peco Setrack Unifrog using a PL-33

PL-33 Microswitch

the frog. This arrangement provides a means of using a Setrack point in live frog mode even when the blades are switched manually by hand.

The above configuration is very straightforward to install (see panel) but some modellers may prefer not to have the microswitch housing visible on the baseboard surface. Therefore an alternative method of auxiliary frog switching (where remote blade operation is being employed) is to fit a Peco PL-13 auxilliary switch directly to a PL-10 series twin-solenoid motor – the wiring being the same as for the aforementioned PL-33.

Above left
Auxiliary switching can be achieved by attaching a Peco PL-13 accessory switch to an SL-10 series twin-solenoid motor.

Above
Auxiliary switching of the frog polarity with the SmartSwitch system requires a SmartFrog.

USING A PL-33 MICROSWITCH FOR FROG SWITCHING ON A PECO SETRACK POINT

1

A Peco Setrack point is illustrated here, together with a PL-33 microswitch (closed type) and PL-19 microswitch housing.

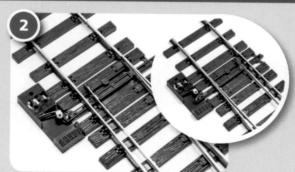

2

The PL-33 microswitch drops into the PL-19 housing, which is then clipped to the sleeper ends either side of the point tiebar. The two views show how the point tiebar activates the microswitch when the blades are switched between the two routes.

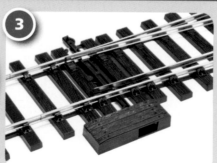

3

There is a cover plate that clips into the top of the microswitch housing, which is designed to resemble a piece of trackside equipment. Painting and weathering will help to disguise it further as part of the layout scenery.

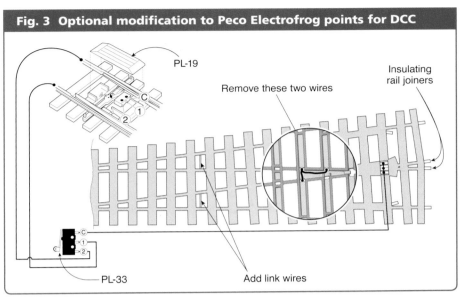

Fig. 3 Optional modification to Peco Electrofrog points for DCC

PL-19

Remove these two wires

Insulating rail joiners

PL-33

Add link wires

Above
All of the Peco Streamline Electrofrog pointwork items (aside from the catch points, crossing and double slip) have a housing between the blades to fit a PL-33 microswitch for auxiliary switching of the frog polarity. The main picture shows the PL-33 in position (but without connecting wires fitted) and inset, with the cover plate replaced.

Peco Electrofrog Streamline two-way points
With Electrofrog points as supplied, there is no 'dead section' as such, since the frog unit is energised through whichever blade is in contact with its corresponding powered stock rail. However, some modellers pefer not to rely on blade contact alone for powering the frog.

An alternative is to use a PL-33 microswitch for which the point is complete with a moulded in-line housing between the blades. The PL-33 fits straight into the housing and once wired up is triggered by the mechanical movement of the point tiebar. This alleviates the need to rely solely on blade contact for energising the frog and is applicable in both manual and remote point operating modes.

Bonding Electrofrog point blades for use with DCC
An issue that can crop up when using Electrofrog points on

a DCC layout is that the backs of wheels on locos with a long fixed wheelbase may glance against the open point blade (which is at the opposite polarity) and cause a momentary short circuit. This can be sufficient to cause sensitive DCC systems to shut down.

To prevent this from occurring, the electrical bonding of the point can be modified as illustrated in Fig.3 and the accompanying step-by-step sequence, such that the polarity of the passive blade is configured to match that of the adjacent stock rail along which the wheelset is running.

The modification entails first cutting the link wire between the frog and the blades on the underside of the point, then cutting a second link wire between the two blades, and finally adding new connections from each blade to its respective stock rail.

Note that this totally isolates the frog unit, so that it must be powered via an auxiliary switch, such as the method described above.

MODIFYING THE WIRING ON PECO ELECTROFROG POINTS FOR USE WITH DCC

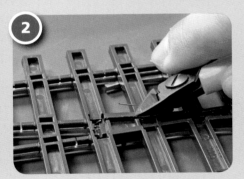

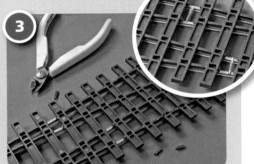

1 Pictured here is the underside of the frog area on a Peco Streamline bullhead two-way Electrofrog point. There are two link wires that can be seen; one electrically bonds the two blades together and the other connects the blades to the frog area. Therefore, as supplied, the blades and frog are all electrically linked as one unit.

2 To undertake the modification, both of these link wires need to be cut and removed completely, for which a set of side cutters are used. The blades are now electrically isolated from each other and in turn from the frog, creating three separate sections. The frog needs to be connected via an auxiliary switch that controls the polarity.

3 Each blade needs to be bonded electrically to its respective stock rail. Side cutters are used to cut away sections of the sleeper base and then short link wires are soldered in place to connect each blade with its corresponding stock rail (inset). Red coloured wire was used here for clarity, but black wire would be much less conspicuous once the track is laid and ballasted.

Fig. 4 Auxiliary frog switching on a double slip

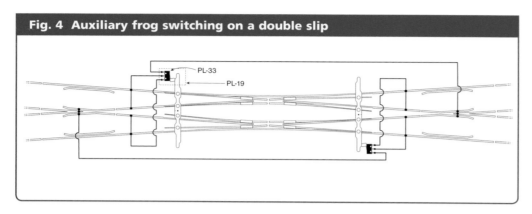

PL-33

PL-19

Peco Streamline Electrofrog double slip

The two frog sections of the double slip need to be equipped with switches to change their polarity. This can be achieved in a number of ways: The method recommended by the manufacturer, however, is to use a pair of PL-33 microswitches in PL-19 housings, with one clipped onto an end of each tiebar. The wiring is then completed as per Fig.4. This method is equally suitable for manual blade operation (i.e, by hand or wire-in-tube) or for use with point motors.

Ballasting O gauge track

In contrast to the items available for N and OO, foam ballast inlays are not part of the Peco O gauge range. Therefore ballasting in this scale needs to be undertaken with loose chippings (such as the ballast granules in the Peco Scene range), applied after the track has been fixed down.

It is possible to glue the track in place and ballast all at the same time, but for best results it is recommended that a three-stage process is adopted – firstly the track is fixed

to the board; then the electrical connections are installed and thoroughly tested; and only then is ballasting carried out; any issues that occur afterwards will be sure to be a result of either stray ballast granules or the glue used to hold the ballast in place. Platforms (or at least the platform faces) should also be in position prior to ballasting.

Streamline track can be pinned or glued with waterproof PVA directly to the baseboard surface, although some prefer to incorporate a sub-base made of thin (3mm/4mm) cork sheet, the purpose of which is to quieten the running, especially on plywood baseboards. The cork also helps to provide a prototypical ballast shoulder at each side.

Ballast granules are available from many different suppliers and are usually offered in a range of grades and colours. The Peco Scene range includes grey and brown ballast granules, available clean or weathered, and in fine, medium and coarse grades. Other materials from the Peco Scene range can also be used to add variety to the appearance of ballast and trackwork, such as the Road Grey scatter (ref.PS-1), Ash & Cinders (fine, medium and coarse grades available) and Sand Load (PS-344).

Above
To change the frog polarities on the double slip, the sleeper base is designed to enable PL-33 microswitches to be used, housed in PL-19 casings that clip directly to the ends of the tiebars.

Below
There is a wide variety of different materials available in the Peco Scene range that can be used for ballasting trackwork. This section of code 143 flatbottom wooden-sleepered track has been ballasted using Peco Scene weathered coarse grade grey stone (PS-307).

Chapter 7

Locomotive & rolling stock modelling projects

The growth of ready-to-run support for O gauge that has occurred in recent years means that modellers working in 7mm scale – once the preserve of the kit- or scratch-builder – have a wealth of proprietary locomotives, coaches and wagons to choose from, to suit both steam and diesel eras. Whether you are looking to model a Western Region diesel depot in the 1970s, or a Colonel Stephens-esque light railway set in pre-Grouping times, there are 'out of the box' models available from manufacturers including Heljan, Dapol and Minerva Model Railways.

However, whilst the ability to obtain suitable ready-to-run stock is a huge advantage to modellers – particularly those new to the hobby or with lesser experience – proprietary models can't match the personal satisfaction of items created as a result of hands-on modelmaking projects. This can be countered by undertaking some level of customisation on your mass-produced models, to make them different to everyone elses – this can be as straightforward as adding an engine crew to a locomotive or weathering a rake of wagons.

Despite the wide selection of R-T-R O gauge models that

have been produced in recent times, there are likely to be occasions when there aren't items available that match your specific needs; perhaps a locomotive isn't available with the running number you require, or a coach isn't available in the livery to suit the era you are modelling. For these situations, there are plenty of suppliers that specialise in transfers, together with etched name and number plates, to assist modellers with changing the identities and liveries of proprietary models.

Aside from the ranges of proprietary models, O gauge modellers are well served by numerous manufacturers offering an extensive array of kits for all sorts of locomotives and rolling stock items. Unless you are after an item that is particularly esoteric, you are likely to be able to find a kit for the specific prototype you are after, whether that be a North British 8T 'Jubilee' coal wagon, LMS clerestory coaching stock, or an Andrew Barclay 0-4-0ST.

Over the succeeding pages we present a selection of modelling projects that cover the tasks commonly associated with O gauge locomotive and rolling stock models, together with an example of plastic wagon kit construction to encourage modellers to have a go themselves.

Above
Pictured here are the finished models from the three step-by-step constructional features that form the basis of this chapter. Also illustrated are various tools and materials that would be useful additions to any modeller's workbench – these include; a cutting mat, steel rule, engineers' square and a modelling knife.

Project 1

Customising a ready-to-run steam locomotive

T he Peckett Class E 0-4-0ST is one of several prototypes to be manufactured as a ready-to-run model by Minerva Model Railways. This characterful industrial design saw widespread use across the UK from the turn of the 20th Century through to the 1960s. With its short wheelbase and small overall dimensions, it is ideal motive power for the compact industrial schemes that are so beloved of many 7mm modellers.

The beauty of using a ready-to-run model as a starting point for a customisation project is that you can choose to do as much or as little as you like, depending upon the finish you wish to achieve and the confidence you have in your own modelling ability. However, carrying out any degree of personalisation on a ready-to-run model will prove to be very rewarding; it sets your model apart from everyone else's and allows you to admire it proudly and think, "I did that!".

The Minerva model offers plenty of scope for personalisation and detailing; indeed, the Peckett is supplied with various 'extras' to be fitted by the modeller if desired. Some amount of weathering – even just painting the shiny wheel rims and bright red injector pipework – helps to give the model a more realistic appearance. However, going further and adding a crew, lamp irons, number plates and other details – as demonstrated here – can really set the model apart from others and give it some individuality.

The best known examples of the Class E Pecketts were the seven originally owned by the Swansea Harbour Trust, which were absorbed into GWR stock following the 1923 Grouping. Some passed into BR ownership, Nos.1143 and 1145 surviving until 1960 and 1959 respectively.

There were detail differences between each of these locomotives, so research is essential when choosing a par-

ticular example to model. This model was finished as GWR No.968 (Works No.1105, built 1908, formerly SHT No.12), the prototype that could be considered the closest match to the Minerva model as supplied.

Top
The finished model that forms the basis of this project, which took just a couple of evenings to complete.

Right
The model as supplied, presented in plain green and sporting the standard Peckett dome. Plain black and lined green versions have also been produced by the manufacturer.

Above
A rare portrait of No.968 under GWR ownership, taken at Swansea in 1937. Of particular note are the original injectors and the toolbox located just forward of the cab. Sporting post-1934 GWR plain green livery with 'shirtbutton' monograms, it is unclear from this view whether the cylinders were painted green or black and also whether the locomotive number was painted on the buffer beams in the traditional Swindon manner – can any RM readers shed some light on this? This photo provided the main reference for the model. *Photo: GWR 813 Fund collection*

The locomotive was dismantled to enable the body and chassis to be worked on separately; this required six screws to be removed from the underside of the chassis. (Part of the foam packaging tray was used as a cradle for the upturned model.) The cylinders were tackled first, for which a representation of the drain cocks and fittings visible on the prototype was fabricated. This was achieved by using brass strip and some spare Ratio 4mm downpipe wall brackets. The latter were seated into holes drilled with a pin vice (*inset*).

It was decided to represent another feature of the prototype, namely the spring tops visible between the mainframes. Some leftover chassis parts from a Parkside Models O gauge wagon kit were found in the 'spares box', which were modified to suit. Owing to the shape of the chassis block on the model, only one half of each of the rear pair of springs was required. Impact adhesive was used to fix them in place.

The chassis was then painted and weathered using a range of enamels (mainly matt black, red oxide, brown and metallic grey) mixed to suit in a clear tray with thinners. Firstly, the wheel rims were then painted, taking care not to let the paint stray onto the running surfaces of the wheels – a cotton bud dipped in thinners can be used to clean the wheel treads after painting if required. All of the motion was painted a dark oily colour (except the piston rod which was left shiny) with gloss varnish brushed on afterwards to complete the oily look. The ashpan was picked out in a slightly lighter, rusty colour. Reference to archive colour pictures is really useful for this sort of work.

4 BR era photos show No.968 (BR No.1143) with a square recess in the back of the cab. The aperture was carefully marked out in pencil, judging the dimensions from photographs. Holes were drilled in each corner and then each side was carefully scored until the waste plastic was removed. After cleaning the edges of the aperture with a needle file, a pair of doors was cut from a section of styrene, fixed to the inside of the cab.

5 The Minerva model is supplied with a choice of three domes – No.968 was equipped with Salter safety valves and bonnet. Whilst the dome cover is a clip fit into a recess in the top of the saddle tank, the feet of the safety valves require holes to be drilled to accommodate them. Similarly, the bell needed a hole in which the spigot could be fixed. The location was determined by using a broadside prototype view.

6 A similar palette of enamels was used to weather the locomotive body. To define the rivet detail small areas were painted at a time with a dark grey colour (thinned to a wash) and then a cotton bud was used to remove most of the paint, leaving traces of paint around the surface details. The cotton bud was drawn in a downwards motion to simulate how dirt and staining appears on real locomotives. As well as the buffer beams, this technique was also used on the cab sides and saddle tank.

7 Before reassembling the locomotive all of the injector pipework was painted black and then touches of metallic copper enamel were brushed on. The toolbox supplied with the model was then fitted in place, located on the left-hand side immediately forward of the cab, as per prototype photos. The toolbox is supported on two battens, which were fabricated from short lengths of Evergreen plastic strip.

8 Usefully, the etched details supplied with the model include a selection of lamp irons. These were cut from the fret with a Stanley knife and then folded to shape using fine-nosed pliers (a set with smooth, not serrated, jaws). Using prototype photos as a guide, the lamp irons were fixed in place using tiny spots of cyanoacrylate.

9 Provided is a choice of five pairs of etched Peckett & Sons builders plates, which are fully legible. These and the cabside number plates (a choice of six numbers is provided) were painted with black enamel and then the raised surfaces were polished with very fine grade wet and dry paper (*inset*).

10 Locomotives in the larger scales look particularly odd when running on layouts seemingly with no-one at the controls(!), so a driver and fireman were obtained from Modelu. These 3D printed figures are based on laser scans of real people and therefore they are extremely convincing anatomically. Supplied in the firm's customary red finish, the figures were first painted black all over and then progressively lighter tones were brushed on for the clothes and features, leaving the darker tones to remain visible in the folds and creases. For the skin colour white was mixed with red oxide and a touch of grey.

11 Suitable transfers for the GWR 'shirtbutton' monograms and power classification/route availability discs were obtained from Fox Transfers; sets ref.FRH7101 and ref. FRH7105 respectively. Once in position, a sparing amount of Humbrol Decalfix was brushed on to seal each of them in place. As a finishing touch, some coal dust was sprinkled on the footplate and also underneath the smokebox door.

Project 2

Building a plastic wagon kit

Constructing a plastic wagon kit in 7mm is – in many respects – little different to an equivalent item in 4mm, so modellers 'moving up' to O gauge from OO will find that starting with a straightforward wagon kit project provides an ideal entry point for modelling in the larger scale. Plastic rolling stock kits are produced by a number of manufacturers, including Peco, Slater's and Coopercraft.

The Parkside Models O gauge range of plastic rolling stock kits (part of the Peco range), covers a vast selection of non-passenger prototypes, including open wagons, box vans, guards vans, bolster wagons and horse boxes. Generally speaking, the kits depict vehicles from the pre-Grouping era right through to the 1970s/1980s, which means the range can satisfy the needs of most modellers, aside from those depicting BR Sectorisation and post-Privatisation.

The Parkside Models kit that forms the subject of this article represents a London Midland & Scottish Railway's 20T goods brake van (ref.PS111). The vehicle is slightly more involved than some of the other kits in the range (such as open coal wagons) because it includes lamp irons, handrails, glazing and footboards. However, the fundamental principles of assembly are common to all of the 7mm scale Parkside Models kits.

The majority of the parts in the kit are plastic mouldings, but there is a handful of etched parts for some of the brake gear components; these do not require any soldering so modellers who are perhaps a little wary of working with brass should not be put off building this kit.

Wheels, bearings, sprung buffers, three link couplings, glazing and transfers are all included, together with lengths of plastic and wire to form the rain strips and handrails respectively.

The black plastic parts are moulded in ABS and the man-

ufacturer advises that this material is not amenable to weaker plastic cements, but that it can be held by ABS cement, superglue or EMA Plastic Weld.

Printed instructions are supplied, with parts numbered and illustrated on a series of accompanying diagrams. Other drawings assist with the position of handrails and construction of the brake gear. Livery information, historical notes and suggested references are also provided.

A nice feature of the Parkside Models O gauge kits is that the boxes in which they are supplied are sufficiently sized to store the completed model.

Over 840 LMS 20T goods brake vans were built between 1924 and 1927 to Diagram 1659. A similar design of brake van – built to Dia.1657 – is already represented in the Parkside range (ref.PS40). However, this design features side lookouts and different verandah details.

An interesting design feature of the prototype, which is reflected in the kit, is the seating of the body on rubber pads, raising it clear of the chassis.

The prototypes bore witness to a number of detail changes over the years so it is advisable to obtain good photographic reference before starting construction. For the model described here, reference was made to the book *Official Drawings of LMS Wagons No.2* by R J Essery, published by Wild Swan (ISBN 1 87410 33 X) which contains drawings and a number of photographs of vehicles to Dia.1659.

Above
After just a few evenings' work the kit is complete; painted, lettered, weathered – and ready for service!

Below
The components as supplied, laid out prior to assembly. Most of the parts are injection moulded plastic, with some brass items.

CONSTRUCTING THE PARKSIDE MODELS LMS 20T BRAKE VAN KIT

(1) The sides need preparing prior to assembling the body; the holes for the handrails are partially moulded and need drilling through using a 0.5mm bit. The instructions suggest fitting the glazing to the inner ends at this stage but it was decided instead to fit the glazing at a later stage of construction, after painting.

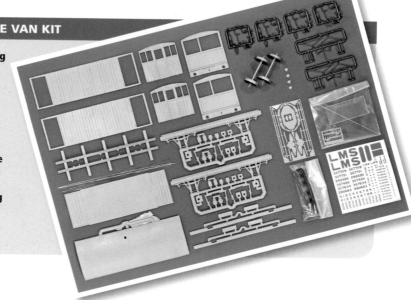

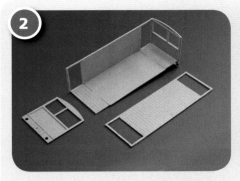

The first stage of assembly is fitting the two sides and two ends to the floor. It is best to work around the floor to try and ensure that three 'good' corners can be achieved. Some careful cleaning up was required to ensure that flash and ejector pin marks did not conflict with any joining surfaces between parts.

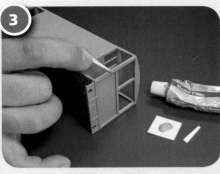

With the inner ends fitted, Humbrol Model Filler was used to fill in any gaps on the corners. Small amounts were applied using the point of a scrap of styrene and, once dry, excess filler was sanded flush with fine grade wet and dry paper.

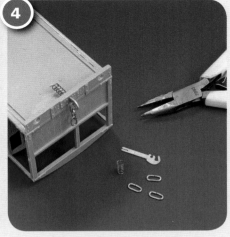

Each coupling comprises a brass hook, spring and three links. Pliers were used to open out the links to connect them together and then the top link was clipped onto the hook, with the brass housing lightly crimped around the link to hold it in place. The hole in each headstock needed to be enlarged to allow the hook to move smoothly. To fit the coupling, the hook was inserted through the headstock and the spring slotted over from the back. Whilst compressing the spring against the back of the headstock, the 'tails' of the hook were bent at opposing right angles to lock the coupling in place.

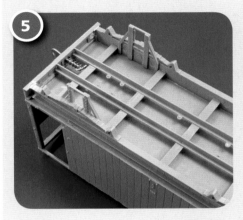

The solebars and sub-chassis were fitted to the underside of the floor. Fillets of styrene sheet were used to fill gaps between the ends of the solebars and the headstocks. Frequent checks were made whilst the adhesive was drying to ensure that the W-irons remained exactly vertical.

The axleboxes are designed to float vertically within the W-irons to offer a degree of compensation when running over uneven trackwork. Two axlebox styles are included, to cater for as-built and later designs (parts for the later design were used on this model). At the top of the picture are the five components that form each axlebox, with a partially assembled example beneath.

The wheelsets are fitted with the axleboxes held in place under tension between the axle ends and the W-irons. It is important to add the wheelsets only once the solebars have dried completely. This is to avoid any tendency for the W-irons to splay out, thereby introducing unwanted 'slop' which could compromise the running quality. It is worth sighting along the length of the vehicle to ensure that the axles are in line with each other. Any small amount of 'rock' can be corrected by adding – to the relevent wheel – tiny shims of plasticard between the top of the axlebox and underside of the spring.

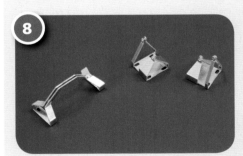

The brass hangers for the brake gear are supplied as etched parts. These can be cut from the fret using snippers and, after cleaning up with a file, folded to the required profiles using pliers. It should be noted that the same etch is used in another kit and therefore not all the parts are required for this model. It is also worth reading through the instructions for the brake gear assembly a few times so that the relationship of all the components can be fully understood.

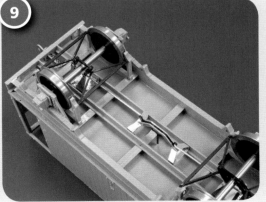

This view shows the completed brake gear in place. The etched parts that support each of the three assemblies are positioned over locating pips on the sub-chassis, enabling ease of alignment. However, the two outer assemblies (that go around the axles) need to be positioned with the component parts 'dry' assembled, which does make for a rather delicate procedure when easing them *in situ*. Only once in place could all the joints be secured with Plastic Weld. A final check was then made to ensure the brake shoes did not bind against the wheel treads.

10 The sprung buffers were assembled and fitted to the headstocks, with small amounts of cyanoacrylate used to lock the nuts in place. The holes in the headstocks may require some reaming out with a file to achieve a satisfactory fit and the insides of the solebars also needed fettling to prevent them from fouling the ends of the buffer shanks.

11 The lamp irons were fitted next. Reference was made to the official drawing published in Essery's book to establish the position of each; note that the lamp irons on the ends are off centre. These were attached with Plastic Weld, using the point of a knife to push them into the softened plastic of the body for a stronger joint.

12 Handrails were fabricated from the sections of 0.5mm brass wire supplied in the kit. About 3mm was allowed at the ends of each one to provide sufficient depth to pass through the locating holes in the model. A scrap piece of 40thou styrene sheet was used as a spacer to maintain an equal distance between the handrails and the body.

13 The fixings for the door bars were added next. Fixing each door bar ring to its respective base is a bit fiddly, the parts being so small. It was decided to omit the actual bars until after painting, otherwise they would be vulnerable to damage and make access to the inner ends with a paintbrush unnecessarily awkward.

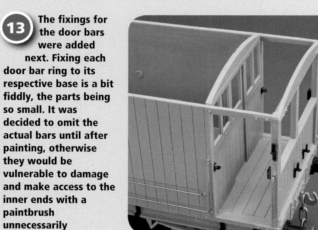

15 It was decided to keep the roof as a separate item until after painting, but the rain strips and chimney were still fitted at this stage. The rain strips were fabricated from the styrene strip provided. To fix each in place, it was first attached with a spot of Plastic Weld at its centre point. Then, working on one side at a time, each end of the strip was eased down towards its respective corner so that it formed its own natural curve. Plastic Weld was then run along the length of the strip to fix it in place (using capillary action to draw it along). When trial-fitting the roof it was discovered that there were gaps around the top curved edge of each end, so strips of 20thou styrene strip were fixed over these top edges to close the gaps.

14 The footboard supports are moulded in ABS, which ensures they are quite robust once fitted. Cleaning up of these supports may be required to ensure they can be seated flush against the solebar faces. It is critical to position the supports exactly vertical and in line with each other so that the footboards will be level when fitted.

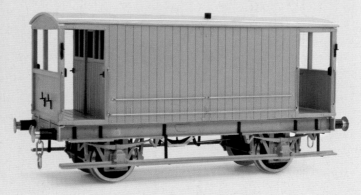

16 The wagon was painted into pre-1936 LMS livery with black running gear, grey solebars and body, white handrails and dark grey roof. Humbrol acrylic was used for the black, but the main grey colour was mixed from artists' acrylics into an interpretation of a slightly faded LMS grey. The works plate on the solebar was picked out in black, with small spots of white added to simulate the appearance of lettering. The floor boards in the verandahs were painted in a bare wood colour.

17 With painting complete, the door bars, glazing and (finally) the roof were added. For the door bars (which were fabricated in a similar fashion to the handrails), three were fitted in the 'closed' position and the fourth hanging down, just to add a bit of variation.

18

Self-adhesive type transfers are supplied in the kit, covering early LMS, late LMS and BR liveries, with a selection of numbers for each. Each transfer is cut round (through the tissue only and not the backing paper) and then picked up and placed in position with tweezers. It is then pressed down on the body before soaking with water. This separates the tissue from the transfer which can then be lifted clear, as illustrated. Photographs in the Essery book were referred to for positioning the transfers, which confirmed that the gap between the LMS letters should be two planks in contrast to the three planks suggested in the diagram supplied in the kit.

19 To weather the model a selection of Humbrol Weathering Powders was used, which helped to define all the plank detail and give the vehicle a realistic 'working' appearance. As a final touch, small amounts of Humbrol Gloss Cote were applied to the buffer heads and spring/axlebox detail to simulate grease and oil.

Project 3

Adding livery details to a proprietary diesel model

Whether you are building an item of rolling stock or personalising a ready-to-run locomotive, it is the application of the lettering and livery details that will really bring the finished model to life. A huge variety of transfers are available from numerous suppliers (including Fox Transfers and Railtec Transfers, to name just two), covering lining, lettering, numbering, emblems, insignia and markings etc. Different types of transfer are available, including waterslide (as used here), rub-down and methfix, each requiring a slightly different method of application.

However, whilst correctly applied transfers can imbue a model with a touch of finesse, mis-placed, wonky or damaged transfers can spoil an otherwise perfectly good model.

The 7mm scale Class 15, produced as a ready-to-run item by the Little Loco Co, is supplied un-numbered and without livery markings. Instead, the manufacturer provides a set of water-slide transfers (produced by Railtec Transfers) enabling the purchaser to finish the model to represent their chosen class member.

Some modellers may be wary of applying these transfers themselves, but the task is in actual fact quite straightforward and, by adopting a few simple tricks, a top quality finish can be obtained with the minimum of fuss.

Above
The sheet of transfers covers all applicable liveries for the Class 15.

Below
D8215 complete. As many photographic references as possible were consulted for accuracy's sake.

ADDING LIVERY DETAILS TO A LITTLE LOCO CO. CLASS 15

(1) Only a few basic tools are required; a sharp modelling knife, steel rule, tweezers, cocktail stick, good quality cotton buds, a small soft brush and container of warm water. Prepare a clean working area before you start, and also ensure that both the brush and water container are clean too; this ensures no dust or dirt will spoil the finish of the transfers.

(2) On this model, the cabside numbers, late BR crests and small warning panels are all arranged as a single decal. Use a steel rule to cut around the required transfer; cut as close as you can without risking cutting through any of the actual printed areas, and be careful not to cut into any of the adjacent transfers.

(3) Submerge the transfer in warm water for a minute or so to release the decal from the backing paper. Use tweezers to extract the transfer from the water and place it onto the model. If the transfer becomes separated from the backing paper whilst in the water, then use a soft brush to pick it up instead – using tweezers risks damaging the transfer.

④

Right
For any model that you are applying transfers to, a good clear prototype photo is an essential visual aid for spacing and positioning. This photo of D8215 was recorded at Stratford on 20 April 1969. *Photograph: Rail Photoprints*

Place the transfer adjacent to its intended location (inset), such that the transfer can be coaxed off of the backing paper directly onto the required location. (It is important to minimise the amount of moving around that the transfer is subjected to as this distresses the carrier film and increases the risk of the transfer becoming damaged or breaking up.) A soft brush, wetted with the warm water, is used to pull the transfer away from the backing paper. Add more water to the transfer if required to help it 'float' into position more easily. The picture shows how the point of the knife is used to pull the backing piece clear, whilst holding the transfer with the brush. If the transfer curls up or folds over on itself, then use the brush to pick it up and place it back in the water, whereupon it will open back out again.

⑤

With the transfer roughly in position, small adjustments can be made using the blunted point of a cocktail stick (the point of the knife is too sharp and risks damaging both the transfer and the model). Keep adding water with the brush if the transfer starts to 'stick' to the model.

⑥ Once happy with the positioning, the excess water needs to be carefully drawn away from around the transfer. A cotton bud is ideal for this but a small amount of tissue can be used equally as well. The soaking up of the water may cause the transfer to move slightly out of position. If this happens, re-apply some water, correct the position, and then dry the transfer again – don't be tempted to correct the positioning after you have removed all the water because this risks damaging the transfer. Leave the transfer to dry naturally and avoid making any contact with it whilst handling the model.

⑦ Other transfers can now be added. The transfers for the cabside numbers on the Class 15 are supplied with just the first two digits in place, with the last two being applied separately according to the modeller's own choice of prototype. When placing multiple transfers together in close proximity to each other, care needs to be taken to ensure that the ones previously applied are not inadvertently disturbed. Spacing the numerals evenly is achieved by eye, but a steel rule is useful for checking they are all in line and level (Inset).

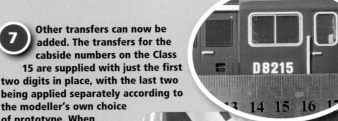

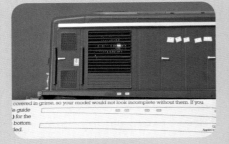

⑧ There are several small markings that are located along the solebar on the Class 15. To aid with positioning, a printed full-size template is provided with the instructions, which is seen here placed next to the

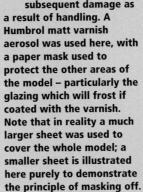

model. There were nine such markings on the left side solebar; two are in place, whilst the remaining seven have been cut out and can be seen temporarily placed on the compartment doors ready to be applied. Creating your own rudimentary templates in this style is a useful method for achieving correct spacing and positioning.

⑨ With all transfers in place it is important to fix them with a light pass of a suitable varnish. This helps to reduce the sheen of the carrier film and, more importantly, protects the transfers from subsequent damage as a result of handling. A Humbrol matt varnish aerosol was used here, with a paper mask used to protect the other areas of the model – particularly the glazing which will frost if coated with the varnish. Note that in reality a much larger sheet was used to cover the whole model; a smaller sheet is illustrated here purely to demonstrate the principle of masking off.

Chapter 8

Modelling the lineside details

Whilst O gauge modellers can take advantage of the growing ranges of fully-finished locomotive and rolling stock models, lineside structures and details are largely the preserve of kit manufacturers. This is not to say that 'ready to plant' items aren't available; a number of painted resin models have been produced by Bachmann (pictured, *inset*) and Hornby for items including diesel fuelling points and signal boxes. Ranges of fully-finished scenic accessories are also available from suppliers including Skytrex Model Railways.

There is a large array of kits available from a number of suppliers for 7mm scale buildings and scenic accessories (of plastic, whitemetal and etched brass construction), catering for layouts depicting all sorts of different eras and geographical locations. However, if a specific prototype location is being modelled, then scratchbuilding may need to be considered, for which detail components and materials are also widely available, including embossed plastic building sheets from Slater's Plastikard.

Peco produces its own selection of O gauge lineside plastic kits and accessories, including tunnel portals, level crossing gates, railway fencing and various station furniture.

In this chapter we have presented a selection of projects that demonstrate the construction of items common to many model railways, such as a small signal box and a diesel locomotive depot. For each of the projects described, only a basic set of tools and materials is required; a sharp modelling knife, a suitable cutting surface (such as a cutting mat), set of needle files and fine grade sandpaper and a metal rule. Additional items may be required for some projects, such as a set of side cutters or small pin vice with selection of fine drill bits.

Main picture
A scene created using products from the Peco range of O gauge kits and accessories, including; LK-733 Single Track Road Bridge Sides, LK-735 Yard Crane, LK-747 Telegraph Poles, LK-743 Flexible Gates and Field Fencing, LK-704 Wooden Lineside Hut and an LK-790 GWR Square Post Signal.

Project 1

Adapting a plastic signal box kit

Right
The packaging illustrates the kit as supplied…

Included as part of the Peco O gauge Lineside range is a kit for a ground level signal box (ref.LK-709). This versatile kit can be built as intended or converted into a full-height structure, as demonstrated here, by creating a brick or stone base, together with a landing and staircase. Such a project bridges the gap between plastic kit construction and scratchbuilding, providing an ideal stepping stone for modellers to progress their modelling skills.

Despite this being a significant adaptation of the Peco kit, the majority of the kit components can be used without modification; the only parts not used being those for the brick plinth and steps.

The kit itself represents a generic design, inspired by a platform-mounted example at Cattal (North Eastern Type S5). For this adaptation, prototype reference was first sought of full-height signal boxes featuring a similar style of cabin to that in the kit. To this end, published drawings of a Hull & Barnsley Type 1 signal box were found in *The Signal Box – A Pictorial History and Guide to Designs* by The Signalling Study Group (published by OPC, ISBN 0-86093-224-9). The drawings catered for timber and BTF (brick to floor) versions; brick construction being chosen here.

Materials required for the conversion were nothing more than some Slater's brick sheet, various oddments of styrene sheet, a few strips of Plastruct and a length of brass wire (for the handrail across the front windows). Further detail can be added to the model by fitting interior detail – and even lighting.

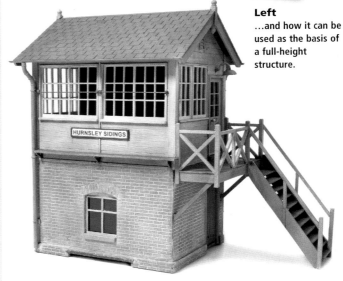

Left
…and how it can be used as the basis of a full-height structure.

ADAPTING THE PECO KIT

1

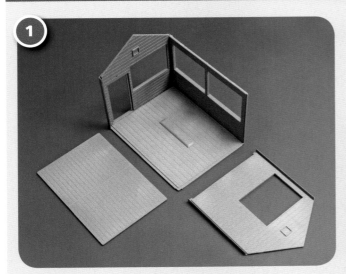

The basic cabin structure was assembled first, which is formed of the five main parts illustrated. The mouldings are nice and crisp, with no cleaning up required aside from removing the burrs where the parts were cut from the sprue. Plastic Weld was used throughout the construction.

2 The roof is formed of just two parts, with separate finials that clip in at each end. It was decided at the outset that the roof would be kept removable; there are locating ribs on the underside of the roof mouldings that help to keep it in position. It was found that the central join along the ridge tiles was sufficient for the roof to hold its shape without any additional bracing. Note that details including the door and windows were not fitted at this stage.

3 The basic cabin structure was used as a reference for measuring out the sides and ends of the brick base onto a sheet of Slater's Plastikard (ref.403). It was calculated such that the base utilised the locating ribs on the underside of the floor that are intended for the brick plinth in the kit. The brick pattern on the sheet used here is stretcher bond, although English bond would probably have been more appropriate. The height of the brick base was set at 60mm, which was based on the proportions of the box in the published drawing. The curved top of the window aperture was scored using a set of dividers.

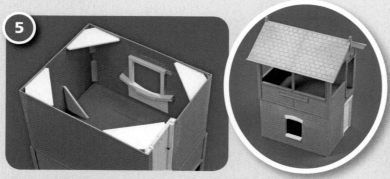

4 The door detail was created from strips of styrene, with 10thou planks applied individually; preferable in 7mm scale than just scoring the joins between planks. The door knob is a Peco track pin, slotted through a pre-drilled hole, secured in place with cyanoacrylate and with the excess snipped off from the back. Bolt and lock detail was simulated using small cubes of styrene. The window arch was built up from the back, with individual bricks cut and overlaid to suit.

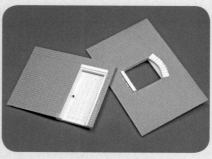

5

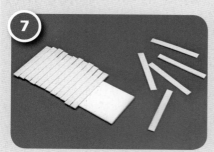
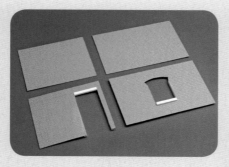

With the basic window and door detail complete, the brick base was assembled (using Wills corner fillets, ref.SSMP199) and then attached to the cabin. Triangular gussets were fixed into the corners and sides, as illustrated, to keep the structure square and rigid. The view also illustrates the internal framework for the arched window. The inset picture shows the overall structure starting to come together (with the roof temporarily placed *in situ* for visual effect).

6

The lower three courses of the walls were stepped out using a lamination of the brick sheet to form a plinth. An oversight was omitting the cut-out at the bottom of the front wall which allows the point and signal rodding to exit the locking room. The front of the model was subsequently modified accordingly, but it would have been much easier to do this prior to assembly of the walls for the base.

7

Attention now turned to the landing, for which a planked floor was first created. A rectangle of 20thou styrene (measuring 66mm x 22mm) was used to support 4mm wide planks applied individually. The planks were deliberately left overlength so that they could be trimmed back to a dead straight edge once they were all in place.

8 The edge of the landing was attached directly to the signal box, utilising the natural rebate that existed between the cabin and the brick base. Vertical posts (31mm long) were added as illustrated using 2.5mm square section Plastruct (ref.MS-100), these being set slightly within the surface of the landing so they were almost flush around the outer edges. The corners of the post tops were rounded off with a file. The gaps between the lower parts of the posts were filled in with sections of 20thou sheet, fettled to a flush fit.

9

The horizontal bars were fitted next using 2mm square section Plastruct (ref.MS-80), attaching them between the vertical posts whilst taking care to keep everything square. For the cross-bracing (also 2mm Plastruct) it is just a case of taking one section at a time and fettling the ends to achieve a snug fit inside the corners – a fiddly process but one which is made so much easier by working in a large scale.

10 For the staircase the steps were constructed first: a strip of black styrene 23mm wide (the width of the steps) was cut first to ensure that they would all match and be exactly in line. Each step was then cut out lengthways from this strip. (The steps in the kit were used as a guide for the width.) The two sideframes were cut next, using the drawing to judge the angle and profile at each end. With one side placed flat, the steps were then added one at a time, positioning them by eye, and using the grid on the cutting mat as a guide for keeping them horizontal. The second sideframe was then attached, cementing it to the ends of the outer steps first, and then working in towards the middle. With the staircase attached to the landing, the posts and handrails were then added using more Plastruct.

A generous amount of glazing material is included in the kit; more than enough to cater for the additional locking room window on the brick base. Each of the upper window frames has two halves, one set back from the other. Therefore each half needs a separate piece of glazing. The apertures were measured and the glazing pieces cut to suit, fixing them in place with Plastic Weld – taking care to avoid getting any solvent on the visible areas. The framing on the lower window was added using 0.75mm square section Evergreen strip (ref.131).

11 Here is the completed structure prior to painting. Note that the windows and door have been temporarily fitted inside their apertures at this stage. The stovepipe was fashioned using a 'T' section cut from part of a sprue in the kit. The drainpipes were fitted next, extended downwards using 2.4mm diameter Plastruct rod (ref.TBFS-3). Note the stepboard along the front of the box which was fabricated from styrene; these were a feature of many full-height signal boxes, providing the signalman with a means of access to clean the outsides of the windows.

12 Painting was completed prior to glazing and fitting of the windows and door. The colour scheme is based on the BR North Eastern Region style; blue and off-white with orange enamel signs. Artists' acrylic paints were used, mixed to suit. For the brick base the original colour of the Plastikard was retained, with a suitable mortar colour brushed on, wiping off the excess almost immediately to leave the residue in between the brick courses.

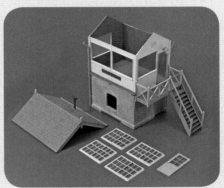

14 The structure was given a dusting of Humbrol weathering powders (mainly Dark Earth ref.AV0007) and then the windows and doors were fitted in place. The nameboard (which is moulded as part of the cabin front) was measured and suitable lettering to the exact size was created on computer using Adobe Photoshop software. The name 'Hurnsley Sidings' is fictitious, with Hurnsley being derived from Hull & Barnsley. Finally, the handrail across the front windows was added using fine brass wire, fitted to styrene fixing points with tiny spots of cyanocrylate. A late addition (overlooked during the earlier stages of construction) was the angled supports underneath each end of the landing, which were duly fitted and painted to suit.

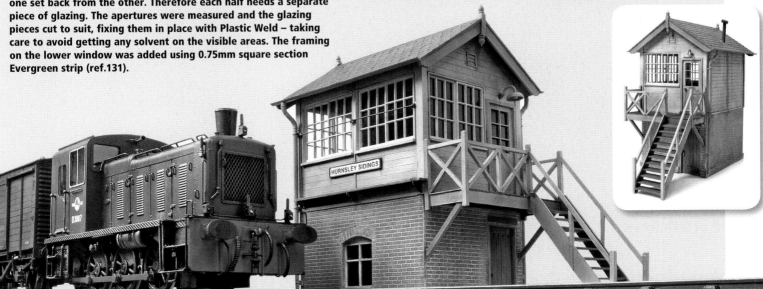

Building a BR Traction Maintenance Depot

The Danish model railway manufacturer, Heljan, has amassed a large range of ready-to-run British Railways diesel locomotives in O gauge. As an ideal scenic accompaniment to them, the manufacturer has also developed a kit for a two-road Traction Maintenance Depot.

Standing 225mm tall and with a footprint measuring a massive 605mm x 305mm, the depot is undoubtedly one of the largest plastic structure kits ever produced for the British model railway market. However, despite its monstrous proportions, the model is actually very easy to assemble and well within the capabilities of modellers of lesser experience.

The design features a red brick base, with extensive glazing panels on the sides, ends and roof, together with concertina rail access doors. Inspiration for the kit was taken from the depot structure at Shirebrook and is representative of a style adopted by British Railways in the 1960s and used extensively across the Eastern Region. Structures to a similar design could be found at locations including Frodingham, March and Tinsley.

The main depot kit (ref.9500), which forms the basis of this project feature, includes sufficient components to build a two-road structure of

the dimensions quoted above. Eight side modules are provided (four per side), together with two 'open' ends and one 'closed' end. The provision of the two 'open' ends enables a through shed to be constructed if desired. Being modular, the kit could also be adapted to form a half-relief structure eight side modules long, or a four-road depot two side modules deep.

There are also two supplementary kits that provide additional components that can be used in conjunction with the main kit, thereby opening up further possibilities with the configurations that can be achieved: ref.9501 comprises four side modules and can be used to extend the length of the main depot kit, whilst ref.9502 comprises two 'open' ends and one 'closed' end.

Despite its size, assembly of the depot can be undertak-

Below
The Heljan TMD kit provides an ideal setting for the extensive range of 7mm scale ready-to-run diesel models that have been produced, such as the Heljan *Falcon*, Class 31 and Dapol Class 08 models pictured here.

en with just a handful of basic modelling tools. A set of side-cutters is useful for cutting parts from the sprues (although a Stanley knife can be used instead), whilst a set of needle files and selection of fine grade sandpapers is needed for cleaning up of the parts. Liquid polystyrene cement can be used to join the main parts of the structure (applied with a small paintbrush), with impact adhesive for fixing the glazed pieces in place.

Right
A representative view of the different sprues included in the main depot kit. Multiple quantities of each are supplied, as indicated on the photo.

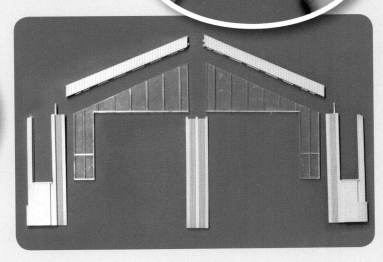

CONSTRUCTING THE DEPOT

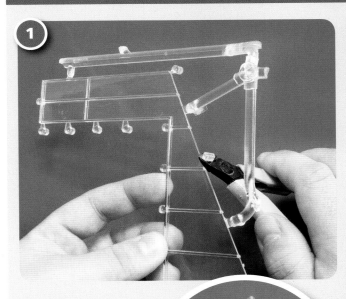

1

2

Here are all the parts for the 'open' end laid out prior to assembly. The inset photo shows how the top roof parts interlock together to form a strong join.

The suggested order of construction starts with the 'open' end of the depot structure with the concertina rail access doors. Components are cut from the sprues using side cutters; particular care is needed with the clear mouldings, which are moulded in a very brittle plastic and prone to cracking. Any remaining traces of the sprues can be cleaned off using a needle file (*inset*).

3

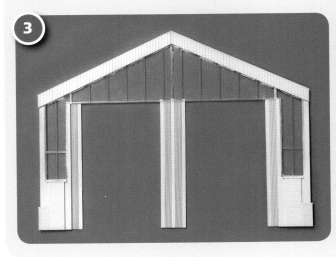

The completed end. EMA Plastic Weld was used throughout, applied with a fine paint brush (*inset*), with impact adhesive used for fixing the glazing parts. The fit of all parts is very good, with no fettling or excessive cleaning required.

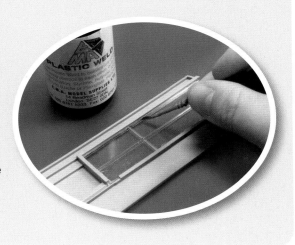

4

Attention now turns to the 'closed' end of the depot. The mouldings with the personnel doors have to be modified for this end of the depot, with the concertina door parts being cut off (*inset*). There is a groove in the reverse of the moulding to identify where this cut needs to be made. The second inset photo shows the completed end.

5

With both ends finished the sides are prepared next. A pair of mouldings makes up each two-bay module, with eight modules required in total (four for each side). The side and roof mouldings lock together very positively, with the correct angle being set automatically.

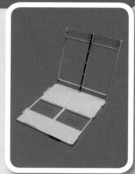

6a

6b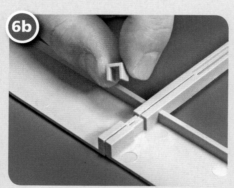

6c

Each side of the depot is created by joining together four of the modules. Photo (a) shows the substantial tabs along the the roof edges that enable the modules to interlock, reinforcing the intermediate joins. Photos (b) and (c) show the additional clips that help to brace the vertical joins that are made at the intermediate pillars.

7

With the side and end elevations ready, the next task is to assemble them to create the shell of the structure. The solvent needs to be applied quite liberally to the insides of the joins to ensure they are as strong as possible. The main photo shows the completed depot shell, prior to fitting of the glazing. At this stage of construction the large size of the model starts to become apparent.

8

On the whole the assembled depot shell exhibits a good level of strength and rigidity. However, the central partition between the pair of rail-access doors is quite vulnerable, it only being held in place by two small spigots at the top. Therefore the join between this partition and the top of the depot frontage has been braced from the back using lengths of Plastruct 'I' girder (ref. BFS-8). The inset photo shows a fillet of styene being fitted to the front of the facade, this being in keeping with the style of prototype structures whilst also disguising the otherwise visible join in the glazing.

Once the glazing parts for the roof skylights are fitted in place, the roof walkways can then be added. The inset photo shows how the parts for the walkways feature numerous locating pips to aid assembly.

The glazing parts could be fitted next, starting with those along the side walls; it should be noted that the rebates on the top and bottom of these glazing parts are different and care should be taken to ensure they are orientated correctly. The study of prototype pictures confirms that the glazing on these structures was far from clear, with glazing of a 'frosted' appearance being fitted from new. To replicate this effect a very fine grade wet and dry paper was used, together with a fibreglass pencil, to distress the reverse of of the glazing parts (*inset*).

With assembly of the kit completed, strips of styrene are used to cover the gaps in the brickwork, with Humbrol model filler used to conceal the joins in the pillars and roof. A length of Plastruct styrene angle (ref.AFS-6) is used to cover the join along the pitch of the roof.

The depot was painted using Humbrol enamels. Starting with the glazing panels (working on one at a time), firstly a dark brown/grey colour was mixed, with some thinners added to reduce the viscosity. This was then painted over the entire glazing panel (a). Almost immediately tissue was used to wipe off the majority of the paint (b). This left residual paint in all the recesses, replicating the natural build up of dirt inside the window frames that occurred on the prototypes. Next the raised surfaces of the glazing bars and frames were painted to suit (c).

After all the glazed panels had been painted, the rest of the structure was painted using a grey-brown palette of colours, together with Humbrol enamel No.82 for the brickwork and No.99 for the yellow on the concertina doors. To finish, the model was dusted with Humbrol weathering powders to bring it all together. There is huge scope for further detailing of the depot – particularly the interior. Additional external fittings that could be considered include a clock on the outside of the 'open' end, personnel door handles, signs and notices, and spotlights.

Project 3

Modelling trees in 7mm

Modelling, words and photography by Gordon Gravett

Trees are an inherent part of most landscapes and consequently form an important aspect within the scenic work on many layouts. Whereas there are commercial products available for 7mm scale, these are largely hand made to order so it is often down to a modeller to produce their own. This does, however, present the opportunity to model specific trees for a scene and also to include character and details more appropriate to a larger scale. It is also modelling that is refreshingly different from the more technical aspects of the hobby and one that gives every opportunity to really bring a layout to life.

When modelling in any scale the height of a tree, if modelled in isolation, could be quite considerable – typically, it might be the height of a bogie carriage on end! Most layouts, however, involve a certain amount of foreshortening so, reducing the height of trees, can help to keep things in proportion and generally help with the visual balance.

Having known them for all our lives, we assume that we are all familiar with trees but it is not always wise to rely on memories alone; some form of reference material – ideally a clear photo – is ideal, and it is often surprising how the character and shape of an actual

tree is far more interesting than we might have imagined it to be. With the ability to resize images on a computer, it is also relatively easy to print out a copy of a favoured subject at the size it is required for the model so that a true size reference is always to hand.

Forming a wire armature

The generally accepted method of producing the basic (or even more complex) structure of a tree is to use a number of wires twisted together so as to give the diminishing size of the branches and the increasing amount of twigs. We call this the armature. Using multi-strand wire is an accepted method but I've always struggled with this. It involves working from the trunk upwards, but as the bunch of wires gets divided, re-twisted and divided again, it is very difficult to gauge how tall or how much spread the eventual tree will have. I know that trees could, in reality, be any shape but my results were not at all pleasing.

My preference now is to work with single strands of soft iron florist's wire and start at the top of the tree and work down through the separate

MODELLING TREES IN 7MM SCALE

1 Photographing an appropriate tree, rather than relying on imagination or memory, is a good starting point for producing a model. This is an oak photographed during the winter to clearly show the branches and, ideally, would be accompanied by a summer photo of the same tree to show the foliage.

2 Soft iron florist's wire. This brand has a fine paper covering which we can use to advantage later when brushing dilute PVA glue over the entire armature.

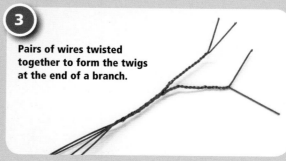

3 Pairs of wires twisted together to form the twigs at the end of a branch.

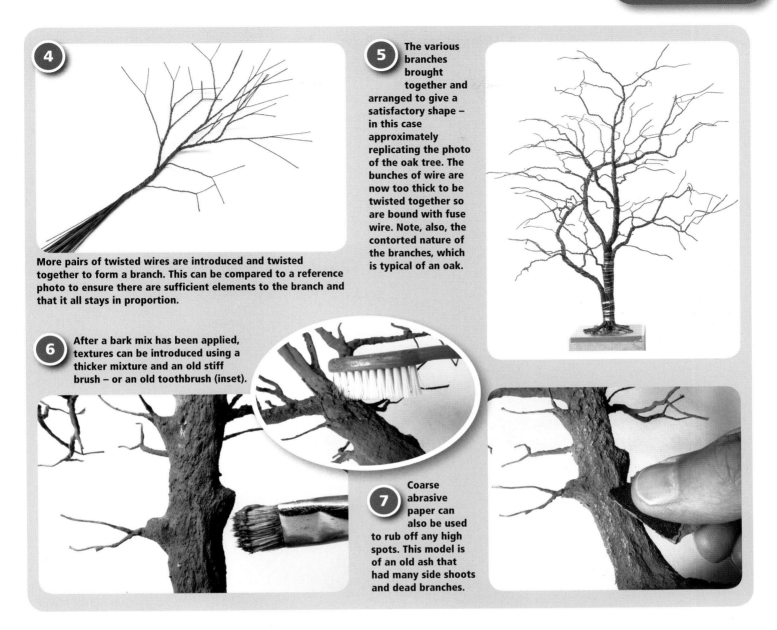

4 More pairs of twisted wires are introduced and twisted together to form a branch. This can be compared to a reference photo to ensure there are sufficient elements to the branch and that it all stays in proportion.

5 The various branches brought together and arranged to give a satisfactory shape – in this case approximately replicating the photo of the oak tree. The bunches of wire are now too thick to be twisted together so are bound with fuse wire. Note, also, the contorted nature of the branches, which is typical of an oak.

6 After a bark mix has been applied, textures can be introduced using a thicker mixture and an old stiff brush – or an old toothbrush (inset).

7 Coarse abrasive paper can also be used to rub off any high spots. This model is of an old ash that had many side shoots and dead branches.

branches. I start by twisting a pair of wires together to form a pair of twigs on a short twisted stem but leaving the 'tails' long. And, then another separate pair is made the same way. These two pairs are then twisted together and, maybe, a third pair introduced a little down from the top. A number of these are made this way and then twisted together to form one larger branch. The process can then be repeated to produce a number of branches, which can be bent, shaped or twisted and, in a procedure not dis-similar to flower arranging, positioned to give the best arrangement or to follow, as best as possible, a reference picture.

With all these wires being brought together the thickness of the branches will grow quite quickly so I usually prune back (to the base of the last twist) about a third of the long 'tails' as I progress. It might also become too difficult to twist all the wires together so, if this is the case, I bind together them with thin fuse wire instead. This is then continued until, eventually, the trunk is formed.

At the base of the trunk, wires around the outside are splayed out and twisted together in twos or threes to form the visible tops of the roots. The central core of wires are

then twisted together to form a spigot with which to locate and hold the skeletal tree on an individual base – with the roots helping to hold it upright. I mount mine on a wood block with parcel tape across the top to prevent anything sticking to it. There is usually some tweaking or trimming to be done to get the desired shape and this, along with the following work and detailing is much more feasible if the whole thing is easier to handle.

Rendering the bark texture

The florist wire I use is paper covered so my next procedure is to brush dilute PVA glue over the entire tree. This seeps in amongst the twisted wires and helps to bond the whole together. It also acts as a base coat for the bark mixture that follows. It helps if the bark mixture has some flexibility and products are available from Green Scene (Flexi-Bark) and Treemendus (Bark Powder) but it can also be made at home.

I mix Artex powder into PVA glue and add a touch of black powder paint to produce a brushable grey paste. Hard plasters (such as Polyfilla) are likely to crack and crumble away. I start with a fairly thin mix to brush over all

8 The trunk of an old ash tree showing many colours for reference and (inset) how the splattered colouring was replicated by flicking paint off an old toothbrush.

9 A winter photo of an oak tree showing the mass of ivy and side shoots growing on its trunk and (inset) the stems of ivy being applied to a model oak using strands of plumber's hemp.

10 Many trees exhibit side shoots growing from their trunks. I used fibrous carpet underlay on this elm before the tree was painted.

the twisted wire and then, once it's completely dry, add more Artex to make a thicker mix and brush this over the thicker branches and trunk. The trunk may need a few coats – with drying time in between – to build up the thickness, depending on the tree being modelled. Finally, I make an even thicker mix and stipple this on. A stiff brush or old toothbrush is then used to produce the desired bark texture.

Painting

Reference photos will give an indication of the colouring and it is quite likely to be more grey than brown. I invariably start with a spray over of grey primer and then adjust the colour with modelling paints – spraying is easier and quicker on such a complex shape but thinned paint can be

brushed over the primer. Mist coats of green, grey and brown aerosols are also very effective. And, coverage of all the finer twigs is not very critical, as most will be covered with foliage. Some trees have quite distinct patches of discolouration or mosses growing on the bark and these can all add character to the model. Other detailing could also be added in the form of the stems of ivy (I've used plumber's hemp for this) or side shoots growing up from the base or all around the trunk where tufts of a fibrous material like carpet underlay are very effective.

Foliage

With the bare tree now completed and painted it might be tempting to consider one of the winter months in which to base the layout, but on the assumption that the chosen

11 The effect of applying scatter material over the side shoots of this model elm tree.

12

Woodland scenics 'Foliage' mat is ideal for all but the finest of detailed trees. A piece is cut or torn away from the mat and teased out as far as it will stretch without tearing apart (inset).

13

The pieces of teased out foliage are then fixed with PVA glue to the lower branches, starting with the ends of the lower branches and then working up through the tree. Most of the leaves on a real tree grow at the ends of the branches so, generally, there is no need to add foliage in the centre. The teased out foliage is then added to the top of the tree (inset).

14 A completed elm tree. This used postiche as a carrier for scatter material foliage. The effect is much finer but the resulting model is a lot more delicate.

season is a little warmer, it is time to foliate the tree. Woodland Scenics 'Foliage' mat is very effective and also very easy to use. The foam rubber 'leaves' are carried on a fine nylon mesh which can be teased out to give a very airy canopy. I cut it into pieces no larger than about 50mm square, and often a lot smaller, and tease these out as far as they will go – almost to the point of falling apart.

I then work around the tops and ends of the bottom branches and attach it with small dabs of PVA glue. Following this I move up through the tree so that the pieces of foliage overlaps the ones below until the top is reached.

By teasing out the mat as much as possible the tree does not appear too 'heavy' or thick and gives the opportunity to see through it to other features beyond.

An alternative to the foliage mat, to get an even lighter effect, is to use a postiche material that can be teased out incredibly fine (almost invisible) and, once held in place by a fine spray of lacquer, fine scatter material can be sprinkled on to represent the leaves. Another fine spray of clear lacquer (not hair spray, it hasn't got the lasting power) secures the scatter material.

These methods can, of course, be simplified – thicker wire with less branches and heavier foliage – to form more basic trees for background use or, conversely, refined to produce very delicate models that stand much closer inspection. There is tremendous scope in 7mm scale for modelling the finer details and there is no reason why this shouldn't be carried through to the scenic aspects of a layout.

little loco company

We have two objectives at Little Loco Company: to produce the most accurate, full-featured and advanced models at the most reasonable price we can afford; and to give any excess profits we make to preservation groups and societies so we can all continue to enjoy our rich and unique railway heritage.

Using modern, and sometimes unique design and manufacturing technologies, we ensure our models look right and perform perfectly. All you need to create a complete model is included, right down to the decal sheet, and all optional upgrades are literally plug-and-play.

Every component is specifically sourced and modified if necessary. For example, our motors have custom windings for scale speed and our speakers – built in to every model we make – are tuned to maximise their harmonic performance.

All of our models are PluX22 DCC compliant and we have now made intelligent auto-sensing DCC a standard feature on every new model we produce. As modellers ourselves we value the time it takes to make your model yours, so whether it's optional parts, sound, smoke, Scale 7 or anything in between, we already have a solution for it. We don't just make models for you, we are you.

To purchase one of our current models or reserve one of our models in development please visit www.littleloco.co.uk, or visit our Facebook page www.facebook.com/littlelococompany/ to find out what we're up to.

Chapter 9

An O gauge Setrack project layout

Andrew Beard describes the construction of the *Talpidae Plaster Castings* layout – one of the many on display in the permanent model railway exhibition at Pecorama, the popular tourist attraction in East Devon.

The aim of this layout project was to demonstrate what can be achieved using items from the Peco O gauge Setrack range in a space of just 7' x 4'3". It was decided to create a split-level scheme, so to start with we constructed a basic 2" x 1" wooden framework for the lower baseboard, fixing this *in situ* on a supporting leg structure. The framework was then covered with lining paper to act as a base on which to plan the layout.

At the time of construction (late 2017) the Peco O gauge Setrack range comprised four components; left- and right-hand points (for which full-size templates are available), a

curve of 40½" radius (16 pieces form a complete circle) and a straight 15½" long. We photocopied a curve and a straight full-size and printed off several copies and then, armed with all the templates, we started to design the layout by laying out the templates on the lining paper.

The basic idea behind the layout was for a canal with loading area, and industrial buildings. By designing for a dual-level layout we could incorporate more trackwork and more movement in the limited space available. As can be seen in the accompanying constructional photographs, some of the straight track

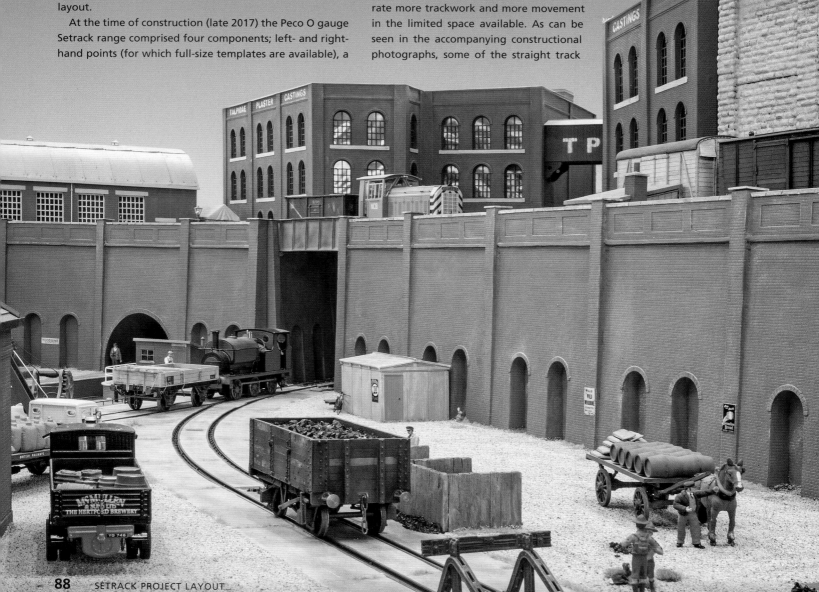

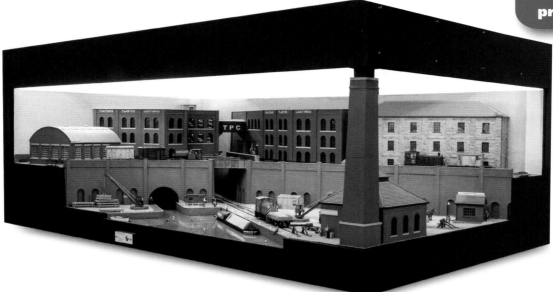

Above
An overall view of the completed layout. Note the push-button mounted on the fascia to activate the swimming ducks animation, and also how the support post in the near corner has been disguised as a chimney.

units were too long for the board area, and so required cutting to length. The layout could have been built using Peco flexible track for the straights and curves, but because the layout was intended to showcase the Setrack items, this is how we proceeded.

With the design finalised, we stuck the track templates in place on the lining paper to use as a full-size reference to assist with construction of the upper level baseboard. The basic wooden shape of the canal barge was also very useful in planning the canal area.

To allow for the canal area we opted to build a raised sub-level for the tracks on the lower level, with many of the supporting timbers at diagonals to the original frame-work. The upper level framework was partly fabricated elsewhere before being secured in place to the corner timbers, with other supports added to give a level surface.

As with many of the layouts in the exhibition, we aimed to incorporate at least one other working feature (apart from the train movements), and with this layout we decid-

ed to incorporate several features such as a working crane, a man reading a newspaper, illuminated lamps – and also ducks swimming on the canal!

Other cameos include a man with a lit cigarette (different times!), which is actually a fibre optic connected to an orange LED, and a man by the canal pumping station who is 'reading' the newspaper (yes, his head really does move – powered by a very slow geared motor). The headline on the back page is most appropriate as 'West Brom win Cup' would place the year as 1968!

Buildings and retaining walls

As many of the buildings/walling required for the layout were not available as commercially produced items, we opted to make our own. Masters were made using foam core board and Slater's embossed styrene sheet, from which silicone rubber moulds were made. The moulds were used to cast all the retaining wall parts required, using fine dental plaster to capture all the detail.

TALPIDAE PLASTER CASTINGS
Overall dimensions: 7' 0" x 4' 0". Each grid square represents 1ft x 1ft

Covered footbridge
Factory
Mill
ST-700
ST-700
ST-700
ST-700
ST-700
ST-700
ST-725
ST-U750
PW
WB
Factory
ST-700
High level track
ST-U751
Hut
Low level track
CS
ST-700
ST-700
Hut
ST-U751
ST-725
ST-700
Factory
ST-725
ST-700
Canal
ST-700
Phone box
Crane
ST-700

Left
A key feature of the layout are the substantial brick retaining walls that separate the upper and lower levels. These were made using modular sections cast in plaster.

Left
This Peco LK-735 crane was motorised using under-board servo motors, operated by a Heathcote Electronics dual servo controller. It swings the load from dockside to woodpile and back at timed intervals, while raising or lowering the load as applicable.

The larger brick buildings are all built around a foam core board shell, with embossed brick styrene sheet glued in place using spray contact adhesive or strong DIY adhesive from a tube. Windows and doors were mostly ones that we cast in resin using our own silicone rubber moulds. To disguise the very visible front support, we built a large brick chimney around it, as part of the pumping works for the canal system.

Finishing details

The lamps are made from Peco kits LK-759, and have been lit using small LEDs with the wires run down through the post to the dc power supply. This facility is allowed for in the kit, but LEDs are left to the choice of the modeller.

The brick built hut is adapted from a Peco kit LK-705, and is actually used to cover a surface-mounted point motor (PL-10 on a PL-12X base) to operate the point. This makes for easy motor repair should this arise, as the hut is removable. We were told by a canal boat enthusiast that no one ever sits with their legs over the side as

Left
This figure smoking a cigarette (illuminated using a micro-LED) is one of many cameos that feature on the layout.

Right
The trio of locomotives illustrated here are ready-to-run items, whilst the wagons are all from kits.

another boat bumping alongside could have tragic consequences, so since these photos were taken our bargee has moved on-board for his tea break!

The layout has a pelmet system around three sides, and onto this at a 45° angle is stuck LED sticky strip on a roll, using warm white and cool white strips to give a pleasing colour.

Extending the plan

For the purposes of automated operation in the Pecorama exhibition, there are two trains – one on each level – that are controlled using a Heathcote Electronics shuttle system. However, if the plan was to be adopted as the basis of a layout at home, it could be extended to incor-

porate off-stage fiddle yards to enable locomotives and stock to be swapped around for more variety, but this need not add more than a few feet in length to the layout. Fiddle yards could be either sector plate or cassette storage system types, and would certainly add to the operational enjoyment.

Oh, and finally – the name of the layout? Well for many years now, regular visitors to Pecorama will have seen myself and my colleague Ian Thompson making and painting moles which are placed around the Beer Heights Light Railway, and which are also for sale in our gift shop. Talpidae is the latin name for a mole!

1 Printed paper templates were used to lay the track plan out full size on a sheet of paper that covered the area of the layout. The grid represents 1' squares. Templates for items of Peco pointwork are available via the manufacturer's website.

2 The framework for the upper level, together with the corner supports, are now in place. The baseboard surface is Sundeala, which is ideal for layouts as it is easily cut and readily accepts track pins. Holes have been drilled in some of the cross timbers for the wiring to be added at a later stage.

3 Hardboard panels have been screwed in place to support the retaining wall sections, whilst backing sheets have also been added for the printed backscene, which will be added at a later stage. Note the operating mechanism for the ducks visible in the canal basin (see separate panel).

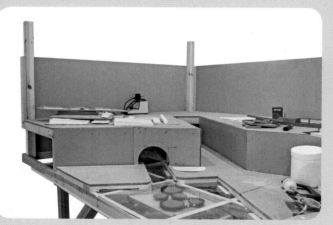

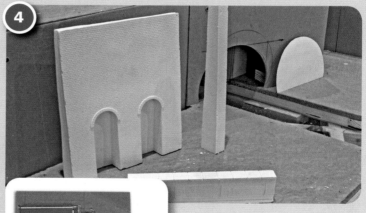

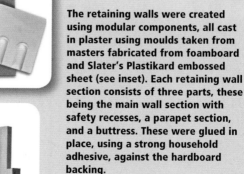

The retaining walls were created using modular components, all cast in plaster using moulds taken from masters fabricated from foamboard and Slater's Plastikard embossed sheet (see inset). Each retaining wall section consists of three parts, these being the main wall section with safety recesses, a parapet section, and a buttress. These were glued in place, using a strong household adhesive, against the hardboard backing.

5

All the retaining wall sections are now in place. The same process was used to create the large stone building visible on the upper level – as described in the accompanying panel. Fascia panels are also in place, together with the substantial corner support nearest the camera.

6

The retaining wall sections (and other areas of brickwork) were painted using Humbrol No.100 enamel as the base coat, with various colour washes and dry-brushed textures being added later to bring out the detail.

7

Track was laid onto ⅛" cork sheet to quieten the running slightly, and also to allow a shoulder to the ballast to form. Sleepering was painted using Humbrol No.84 enamel, and dry-brush weathered, with the rails being painted a rust colour. The points are operated using Peco PL-10 twin-solenoid motors, the one visible here being surface-mounted.

8

We also added a couple of buffer stops with wired-in LED lighting. These are 3mm LEDs which have been fitted to Peco LK-740BH buffer stops by drilling out the lamp and gluing the LED in place. Wiring was completed using very thin multi-strand wire which was carefully run along the buffer stop's sideframes and glued in place, before being painted to disguise it, with the wires being connected to a dc power supply.

9

Ballasting was undertaken using Peco Scene coarse grade weathered brown loose ballast granules (ref.PS-317), secured in place with diluted PVA glue applied with a small pipette.

10

On the lower level, part of the track was inset – as could commonly be seen in dockside areas – and this was made using Wills concrete sheets (ref.SSMP214), which represents this well. Any gaps were disguised with targeted applications of Peco static grass fibres to represent weeds and other vegetation growing between the cracks in the slabs of concrete.

11

To break up the flat expanses of ground around the buildings, grass tufts, static fibres and scatters for flowers were added. All of these items are available as part of the Peco Scene static grass range – the longer fibres (for example 8mm and 10mm) being particularly well suited to applications on O gauge layouts.

SWIMMING DUCKS ANIMATION

1 It was decided to make the ducks 'swim' on the canal, operated by visitors via a push-button mounted on the layout fascia. The first test, however, was to ensure that we could engineer a means of making the ducks move: The canal water surface is thin acrylic sheet, so with a large magnet below the surface and a tiny one above we pushed and pulled the larger magnet to see if the smaller one would follow, which it did. We then sourced some plastic drive chain, sprockets and geared motor drive from a former layout, and these were built into a drive system for the ducks, with the tiny magnet being embedded in the base of each duck. The larger magnet under the canal surface is secured to a steel bolt, which is itself self-tapped into the plastic drive chain (inset). Mass pro'duck'tion of ducks was made possible using a silicone rubber mould taken of our own duck design, with a sufficient quantity cast in resin and painted to suit.

2 A view underneath the layout showing the geared motor (Expo) that drives the sprockets. It is mounted to a substantial timber bracket, with the wires connecting it to a variable 12V dc power supply.

3 The underside of the canal water was painted using enamel paints, but to ensure this would not be rubbed away by the passage of the lower magnet we added a very thin plastic sheet between the magnet and the painted area. Under test it was found that this did not affect the performance of the magnets or ducks. The overall view on p89 shows the fascia-mounted push-button.

CASTING MODULAR BUILDING PARTS

1 The large stone building on the upper level was constructed using modular wall castings. This is quicker than making the whole building from styrene sheet, although the resultant structure is much heavier and therefore this method is only really suitable for permanent layouts. This picture shows the masters for three modular sections, fabricated using foamboard and Slater's Plastikard embossed stone sheet.

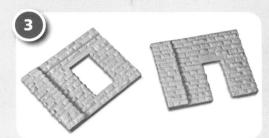

3 Examples of two castings fresh from the moulds. The drying time for each casting does mean that creating sufficient parts for the building had to be undertaken over a period of time, in parallel with other tasks on the layout.

2 Pictured here are two of the rubber moulds taken from the masters. The mould on the left is unfilled, whilst the mould on the right has been filled with the plaster casting compound.

4 A supporting inner shell for the structure was created from MDF, onto which the castings were glued using a strong DIY contact adhesive.

5 With roof, window frame and guttering/downpipe details added, painting was completed using enamels, with dry-brushing to simulate weathered stonework.

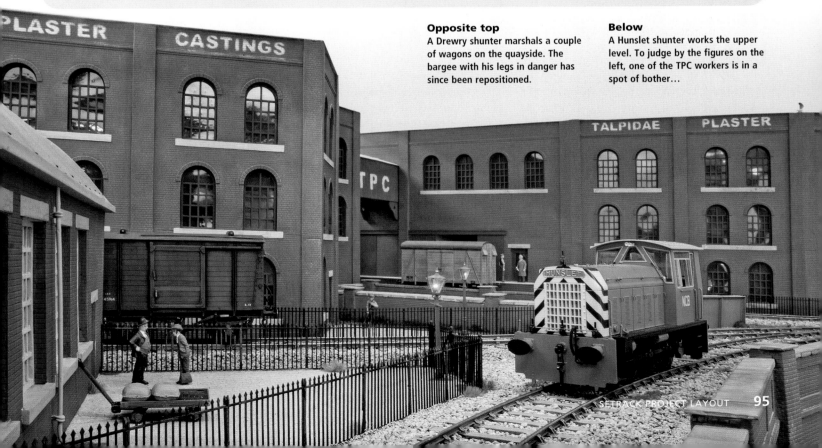

Opposite top
A Drewry shunter marshals a couple of wagons on the quayside. The bargee with his legs in danger has since been repositioned.

Below
A Hunslet shunter works the upper level. To judge by the figures on the left, one of the TPC workers is in a spot of bother...

Gauge 1 & Gauge 3 – modelling in the larger scales

Many O gauge enthusiasts will tell you how 7mm scale locomotive and rolling stock models possess a gravitas – a mix of mass, inertia and presence – which is absent from smaller scale railways. Hold the models, run them, shunt them and you'll experience that special intrinsic quality.

Imagine then how even larger scale models might impact upon your senses. In this chapter we examine and consider railway models built to Gauge 1 and Gauge 3 standards – models which are roughly 1.5 X and 2 X the size of O gauge models respectively.

Unlike O gauge, which has seen a renaissance in commercial support and huge growth in ready-to-run product availability, both Gauge 1 and Gauge 3 modelling is still largely dependent on kit- and scratchbuilding skills, though in recent times an increasing number of manufacturers and retailers have been offering ready-to-run models in Gauge 1.

Both scales have their own dedicated national society which can help newcomers and even established modellers find their way around and provide members with specialist component parts, plans and guides.

Also, if you might suspect that these larger scales would be the preserve of outside model railways, then read on.

Whilst certainly they are both ideally suited to garden lines, indoor layouts on conventional baseboards are entirely feasible too, as we are mostly demonstrating here.

Gauge 1

Starting with the lesser of the two larger scales, Gauge 1 models are built nominally to a scale of 1:32: ie ³⁄₈"/1', or 9.53mm/ft. This has been generally accepted as rounded up to 10mm to 1ft, which actually equates to a true scale

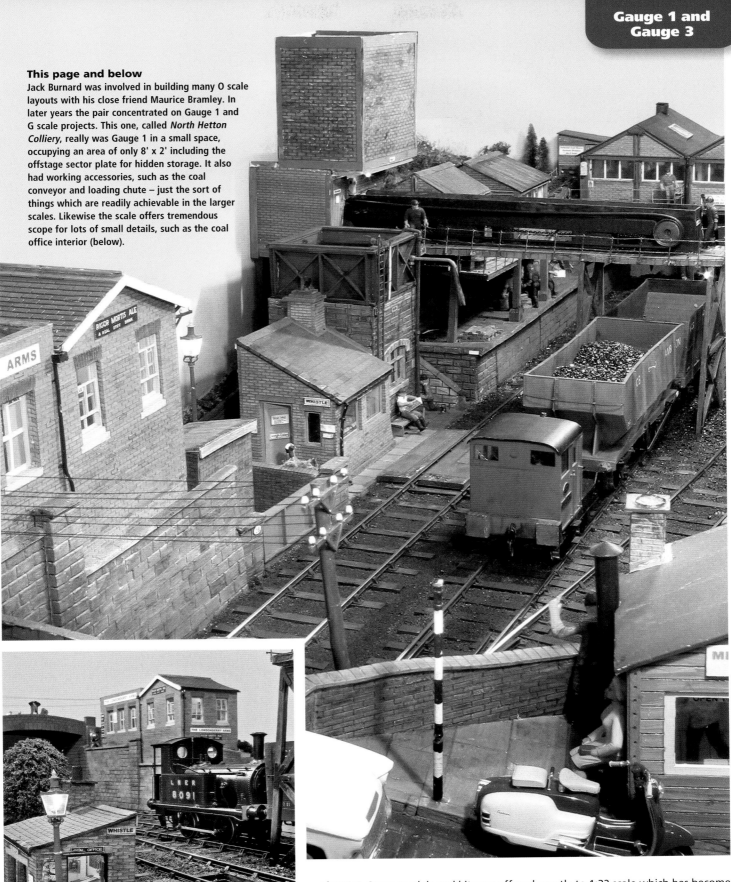

This page and below

Jack Burnard was involved in building many O scale layouts with his close friend Maurice Bramley. In later years the pair concentrated on Gauge 1 and G scale projects. This one, called *North Hetton Colliery*, really was Gauge 1 in a small space, occupying an area of only 8' x 2' including the offstage sector plate for hidden storage. It also had working accessories, such as the coal conveyor and loading chute – just the sort of things which are readily achievable in the larger scales. Likewise the scale offers tremendous scope for lots of small details, such as the coal office interior (below).

of 1:30.5. Some models and kits are offered exactly to 1:32 scale which has become known as ScaleOne32, a similar situation in fact to the small differences between O Gauge and Scale 7.

Both 1:32 and 10mm/ft models use a track gauge of 45mm to represent the British standard gauge prototype. As a rough comparison, Gauge 1 models are one and a half times larger than O gauge models, and two and a half times larger than OO gauge ones. Choosing either 1:32 to 1:30.5 is a matter of personal choice, as both are compatible with commercially available track. Gauge 1 Code 200 bullhead track and LH and RH points are obtainable from the Peco Streamline range.

Above

Maurice Bramley and Jack Burnard were early pioneers with indoor Gauge 1. This layout, *Bamburgh*, was built in the late 1990s and toured exhibitions both in the UK and overseas.

GAUGE 1 MODEL RAILWAY ASSOCIATION

The Gauge 1 Model Railway Association was formed over 70 years ago and has world wide membership. It publishes a quarterly newsletter containing articles on all aspects of Gauge One modelling, including constructional advice for novices and experienced workers alike, plus new product and trade information. New members receive printed details of the recommended Standard Dimensions for Gauge One. A Membership directory plus other useful information is also provided together in a 'New Members' pack. The association also organises national and regional events and members get-togethers. For more information visit the website:

www.g1mra.com

As mentioned briefly in the introduction we are also more likely to find different means of propulsion for the locomotive models; most usually either conventional two-rail electric control, on-board battery power, or live steam. The latter two may include an RC (radio control) means of driving the locomotives, which is becoming increasingly popular for those who build outdoor railways.

As one might expect ready to run models in this scale often come with a premium price tag. This is because the models are not mass produced in the same way that smaller scale models invariably are. A particular locomotive may only be manufactured in limited numbers and assembled and finished by hand – hence a hand-crafted price. That said, it is often possible to buy the same model in kit form and save yourself money, but then it has to be constructed either by yourself, or by a professional model maker which will be an additional cost anyway.

Most of the ready to run products on the British market are manufactured in the far east and are usually available for purchase through numerous British-based firms and retailers. Moreover many are direct sales only via mail order, or at selected shows, and only limited quantities are offered, so pre-ordering is usually recommended, as batches of more popular items can sell out quickly.

Because the firms are small specialist suppliers, it can be something of a labyrinthine task tracking them down individually, but The Gauge 1 Model Railway Society (see panel) has a very good listing of suppliers on its website.

Two of the leading firms offering Gauge 1 live steam models are Aster Co Inc and Accucraft Trains Inc. Based in the US they have British partners –- Aster Hobbies (UK) LLP and Accucraft UK Ltd. At the time of writing (2018) their US counterparts are currently collaborating on new product developments, and both British partners are offering current products for sale in the UK.

For dc and DCC electric powered Gauge 1 models, firms such as Tower Models, Finescalebrass (UK) Ltd., Golden Age Models, Garden Railway Specialists and LH Loveless and Co offer a good selection of R-T-R locomotives, typically express passenger types, though Tower Models does have the smaller shunter types in its portfolio – the L&Y 0-4-0ST Pugs for instance. Ready-to-run coaches and a selection of wagon types are also available from some of the above firms.

Turning to kits in Gauge 1, both loco and stock, these offer entry into the scale for a more modest outlay. There are a number of kit manufacturers to note – many who also produce O gauge kits as well. For example Mercian Models offers a really good range of loco and rolling stock kits, and also a building and finishing service for a selection of its kits.

Finally it's worth noting that several European manufacturers produce Gauge 1 ready to run models of overseas outline prototypes, notably Märklin and KM1 in Germany.

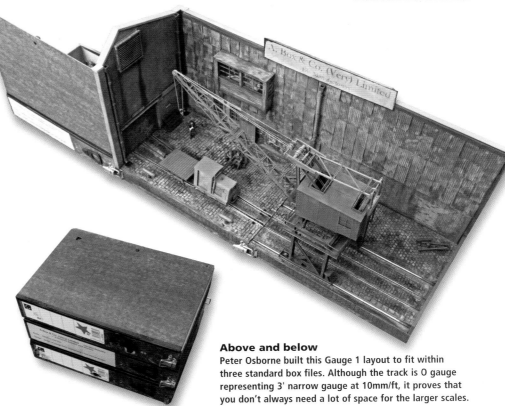

Above and below
Peter Osborne built this Gauge 1 layout to fit within three standard box files. Although the track is O gauge representing 3' narrow gauge at 10mm/ft, it proves that you don't always need a lot of space for the larger scales.

Fig.1 Suggested minimum planning dimensions – inches (mm)

For standard gauge railways

Scale/Gauge	G1
Point length (medium radius)	24 (612)
Crossover (long)	42 (1067)
Minimum track centres	4^1/$_8$ (110)
Minimum radius curves	72 (1830)
Minimum platform width	6 (152)
Min. overhead clearance	9 (229)
Average coach (64')	26 (660)
Typical wagon (10' wb.)	9 (229)

Minimum length of loco release = length of loco over buffers + 10%

Suggested minimum length of headshunt = longest loco + three longest wagons

Note: These dimensions are nominal and meant as a guide for use when sketching out ideas. Always check out your plans with trials using paper point templates, or actual points and lengths of track.

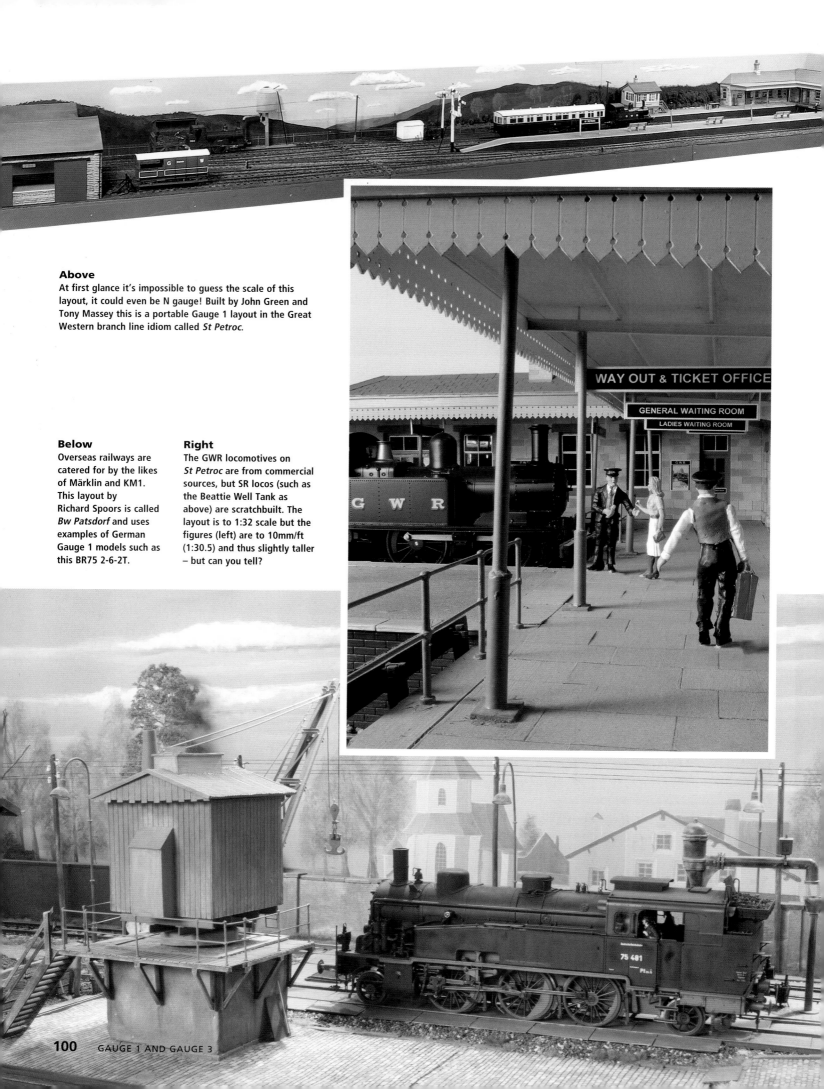

Above
At first glance it's impossible to guess the scale of this layout, it could even be N gauge! Built by John Green and Tony Massey this is a portable Gauge 1 layout in the Great Western branch line idiom called *St Petroc*.

Below
Overseas railways are catered for by the likes of Märklin and KM1. This layout by Richard Spoors is called *Bw Patsdorf* and uses examples of German Gauge 1 models such as this BR75 2-6-2T.

Right
The GWR locomotives on *St Petroc* are from commercial sources, but SR locos (such as the Beattie Well Tank as above) are scratchbuilt. The layout is to 1:32 scale but the figures (left) are to 10mm/ft (1:30.5) and thus slightly taller – but can you tell?

WAY OUT & TICKET OFFICE

GENERAL WAITING ROOM

LADIES WAITING ROOM

Above

Gauge 3 indoors as illustrated by *Blackgang*, an Isle of Wight railways depiction in Southern days by Marc Pretious.

Gauge 3

Gauge 3 has been described as the King of model railway scales: above that size and we are into the realm of true miniature engineering where steam or internal combustion traction power is the norm.

In Gauge 3, low voltage (12V – 24V) electric motors can still provide adequate traction power enabling indoor layouts to be built where sufficient space exists.

Gauge 3 models are built nominally to a scale of 1:22.6: ie very roughly ½" to 1ft, generally rounded up to 13.5mm/1ft in metric. They use a track gauge of 63.5mm to represent the British standard gauge prototype. As a rough comparison, Gauge 3 models are almost twice the size of O gauge models, and nearly three and a half times larger than OO gauge ones.

Although low voltage electric propulsion is common, if you would prefer live steam Gauge 3 out of doors, a few suppliers offering ready to run locomotives live steam exist. The models are however available only to order, rather than off the shelf. Kingscale for example has several Gauge 3 loco designs in its portfolio and its models can be obtained direct or through selected suppliers.

For electric propulsion, Garden Railway Specialists Ltd offer a modest number of Gauge 3 locomotive kits, some of which can be purchased assembled and fully finished. Though again bear in mind that stocks are not huge. Elsewhere you might find the occasional Gauge 3 locomotive kit available in ones and twos, or even second-hand,

GAUGE 3 SOCIETY

Because there is little public and commercial advocacy for Gauge 3, many members believe that the main benefit of joining the Gauge 3 Society is to meet and network with other like-minded enthusiasts and pick up the latest news, hints and tips and discover how others have overcome similar problems.

The society's own journal – The Newsletter – is published quarterly and includes articles, letters, items for sale, illustrations and colour photographs of garden get-togethers, locomotives and rolling stock. Society members also have exclusive access to the Society's shop which supplies track parts and other items at preferential prices.

For more information visit the website:

www.gauge3.org.uk

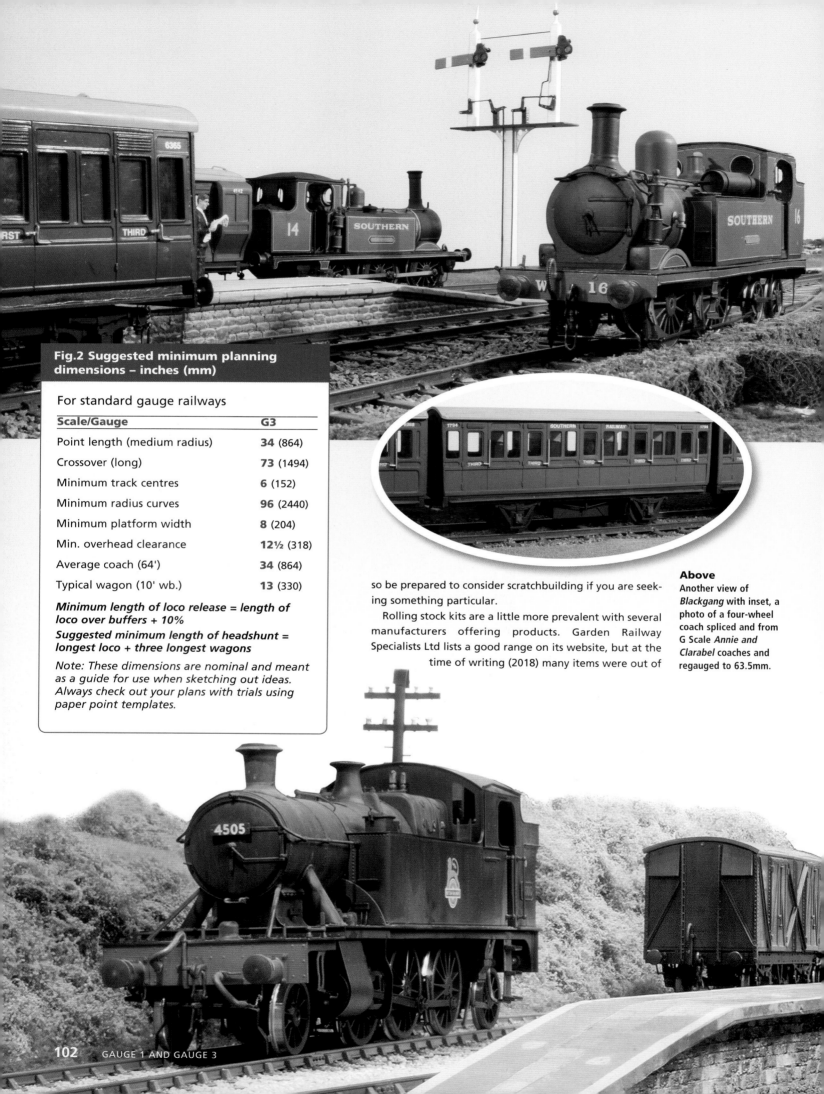

Fig.2 Suggested minimum planning dimensions – inches (mm)

For standard gauge railways

Scale/Gauge	G3
Point length (medium radius)	**34** (864)
Crossover (long)	**73** (1494)
Minimum track centres	**6** (152)
Minimum radius curves	**96** (2440)
Minimum platform width	**8** (204)
Min. overhead clearance	**12½** (318)
Average coach (64')	**34** (864)
Typical wagon (10' wb.)	**13** (330)

Minimum length of loco release = length of loco over buffers + 10%

Suggested minimum length of headshunt = longest loco + three longest wagons

Note: These dimensions are nominal and meant as a guide for use when sketching out ideas. Always check out your plans with trials using paper point templates.

so be prepared to consider scratchbuilding if you are seeking something particular.

Rolling stock kits are a little more prevalent with several manufacturers offering products. Garden Railway Specialists Ltd lists a good range on its website, but at the time of writing (2018) many items were out of

Above
Another view of *Blackgang* with inset, a photo of a four-wheel coach spliced and from G Scale *Annie and Clarabel* coaches and regauged to 63.5mm.

Right
Another view of *St Ives* in Gauge 3 by the late Michael Heaven with a certain Pete Waterman (right) inspecting it at a NEC Warley National Model Railway Exhibition. This clearly shows the relative size of Gauge 3 models in relation to 1:1 scale humans.

stock. Woodbury Models, also a Gauge 1 supplier, offers several laser cut wagon kits to special order. Another Gauge 3 parts supplier, Williams Models, offers several complete kits along with numerous component parts from which its 'flexi-kit' range is derived, allowing many different wagon types to be constructed.

G Scale

As if designed to confuse the hobbyist when it comes to understanding the notion of scale and gauge, there are also models built to G scale standards.

G Scale is actually very well supported commercially, with numerous firms, like Bachmann US and the German firm LGB, producing excellent ranges of R-T-R models and accessories. But G Scale is a hybrid scale: many models and accessories are ostensibly built to a scale of 1:22.5 – very close to Gauge 3 – but run on 45mm gauge track – or Gauge 1 track.

The consequence of this is that whilst many models produced under the G scale banner run on 45mm gauge track,

they may be to different scales completely, such that narrow gauge loco models end up as being larger than their standard gauge cousins.

Many enthusiasts are not fussed by this inconsistency with scale, they simply enjoy the pleasure of running their models straight out of the box.

Of course, if scale authenticity is important to your modelling, G scale may not be for you, but remember that the track is compatible with Gauge 1, and the many accessories – figures for instance – are compatible with Gauge 3. So commercial offerings from G scale may be suitable whatever larger scale you adopt.

Peco produces both flexible and sectional track and points in its Streamline range for G Scale (G-45) with code 250 rail.

The larger scales in summary

In conclusion the larger scales do offer something out of the ordinary, not least models with even greater presence and inertia than O gauge ones. Live steam is a serious option, but with the impediment of increased cost and less variety. If you stick with two-rail electric propulsion you can also integrate all the benefits and features of DCC, though bearing in mind the higher current requirements of these larger models.

Working in these scales can be extremely fulfilling, especially if you like to build things yourself. So don't let the fact that commercial support is not as good as for the smaller scales deter you, if Gauge 1 or Gauge 3, and even G Scale appeals – then go on and give it a go.

THE ASSOCIATION OF LARGER SCALE RAILWAY MODELLERS

Set up in 2000, the Association of Larger Scale Railway Modellers is a group open to anyone interested and working in any of the larger scales; S, O, G1, G-45, G3 and upwards. It is not a replacement for any existing societies, groups, or clubs, but aims to complement them. Its principal aim is the further promotion of the larger scales and it organises various events across the UK. For further information visit the website;

www.alsrm-events.co.uk

The Association of Larger Scale Railway Modellers Limited
President: Lady Judy McAlpine

Scales 7 to 7

All Scales & Gauges between

0 Gauge & 7 ¼

We also cater for S Scale

The Association annual show is in early May, details of which can be found on our web site: www.alsrm-events.co.uk We also try to keep up to date details on UKModelshops web site. We have in excess of 60 traders already signed up for our show in 2019, in addition to these there is a minimum of 15 societies who will be attending the show. This is the largest show of its kind in Britain.

Association members, are entitled to visit the show free of charge, and also included in their membership a minimum of three newsletters are published each year, with occasionally being supplemented with a DVD. A number of traders offer discount on production of a current membership card, these include Slater's Plastikard, MSC Models and others. ALSRM also supports other shows throughout the country.

Membership details can be obtained from
Mark Sanders, 1 Heath Road, Hockering, Norfolk NR20 3HT
Or visit our web site at www.alsrm-events.co.uk

Chapter 11

Garden railway systems

I f you find yourself with limited options for accommodating a large scale layout within the home, or if you wish to adopt live-steam propulsion in preference to traditional electronic control methods, then a garden or outdoor space offers tremendous potential. Aside from the practical benefits of having a larger space at your disposal, bringing your modelling outdoors also enables you to turn what is – traditionally at least – a hobby for the colder months, into one that can be enjoyed all year round; construction and maintenance of the locomotives, stock and structures can be tackled during the autumn and winter months, with work outside on the garden railway and running sessions taking place during spring and summer – weather permitting of course!

A garden railway system also allows you to enjoy your hobby with family and friends, turning what often seems to be a rather solitary pastime into an altogether more sociable pursuit.

This chapter provides an overview of the key considerations for embarking on the construction of a system outdoors – these aspects being universal across the three larger scales covered by this publication.

Design considerations

By way of an introduction it is probably best to start with the track base or baseboard as these are common across the larger scales. When designing a garden railway it is important to take into account the area in which the railway is to be built, taking note of any slopes in the terrain, immovable objects such as sheds, large trees, footpaths etc and to plan accordingly. Firstly it is a good idea to draw a scale plan of the garden area marking in all the above, ideally dividing the plan into 12" squares (or 300mm if you work in metric) to assist with the layout design process. At this stage it is useful to make a number of photocopies on which to sketch some layout designs and ideas.

Minimum track radii must be taken into account at the design stage to ensure the curves will be suitable for the locomotives and stock that you plan to run; the larger the radius the better, as this will allow for smoother running, and avoids stock overhanging on tight curves which can look rather odd. Unless you have a particularly small area to use, a larger layout is better and will give the trains somewhere to go to and return from. Most importantly you will need to decide if the layout is solely for your own use, or will you be hosting meetings for friends to run their trains as well? If you intend hosting meetings, then it is worth considering where all the extra locomotives and stock will be placed and how the layout can be operated with multiple trains in action, so adding some double track or passing loops is almost essential plus of course plenty of siding space for storing rolling stock. The plus side of course is that when everyone else has gone home, you have a more interesting layout to operate. For live steam operation, a steaming-up/servicing area is essential to avoid conflict with trains running on the main layout.

Raised and ground level trackbeds

With a basic plan arrived at it is a good idea to plot out the route in the garden using simple wooden pegs tapped into the ground to give an overall idea of how the design would appear. Of course it is also important to consider at what height you would like your layout to be. Many garden railway enthusiasts have their own preference, whether it be a ground level line or a raised one, and these both have their pros and cons.

A ground level line can blend seamlessly into the garden environment, but can be prone to flooding in low lying areas of garden unless adequately drained. Also the local wildlife will soon take a keen interest in your creation, and will be rooting around in the borders and depositing debris on the line. Of course leaves on the line in the autumn are an issue, but for the determined enthusiast, a quick whip-round with a soft handbrush will soon clear the line for a running session. Another thing to bear in mind with a ground level line is that you will need to bend down quite a bit to tend to your layout and trains, which as most

Above
A dedicated locomotive servicing area is essential for live-steam systems. *Photo: Graham Nicholas*

Opposite page
Combe Down is an impressive Gauge 1 ground-level system.

Below left
Graham Nicholas' Gauge 1 garden railway, *Lincaster* runs on a raised trackbed. *Photo: Graham Nicholas*

Below
Tony Crouch disguised the raised trackbed on his O gauge garden railway using hedges.

of us will testify can be an issue. For a raised line, bending down is not an issue so much, as a different form of construction is required to give a stable trackbed, but at least the garden borders won't end up on the trackbed, although leaves will still cause an autumnal problem of course.

Many gardens are rarely completely level so a combination of ground level and raised trackbed is quite common and can look more natural. Whichever type you choose, it is best to have the steaming up/servicing area at waist height as it is much easier to work on your locomotive.

Trackbed construction

There are many types of base that can be used for the track to be laid on, and it seems that new ideas pop up from time to time as well. For a ground level line some may consider using a concreted base, or breeze blocks laid flat, and these are both ideal where the layout is to be permanent. Fixing the track in place can be somewhat more labour intensive though, as track will need to be screwed down into previously Rawplugged holes which will need to be drilled at regular intervals into the base.

A raised structure is usually, but not exclusively, built of timber. This can take the form of wooden fence posts concreted in place with 2" x 1" tannalised timbers screwed to the side of the posts at the required height to give a skeleton structure for the baseboard. For the baseboard surface decking timber can be used, smooth side up, screwed to the outer timbers.

Other methods of construction that have been used involve stone or brick piers or walls such as on the outdoor layout at Pecorama, while other lines have used steel posts and framework, or even plastic drainpipe for the uprights. Whichever method you use, take your time over construction to get a smooth layout base with no humps and bumps or odd cambers, as this will pay dividends when your track is laid and you start running trains. Returning to the raised construction, the baseboard can be left as it is if you wish or, as many modellers do, you can cover the boards with smooth roofing felt secured at the outer edges with roofing felt nails to give an imitation ballasted look. To neaten up the edges it is best to add tannalised timber strips over the felt edges which helps hold it in place, but also looks much tidier.

Other types of baseboard material that can be used are marine plywood (hard to find and also expensive), and recycled plastic boards made to look like timber boards which of course will not rot. Of all the types of baseboard top, decking timber is the easiest to source and probably the most cost effective. With all of these types of surface, track can simply be pinned in place using brass nails. It is of course possible to add real stone ballast, and we have found that the most long lasting method of securing it is to use exterior grade PVA. The glue is applied neat and the stone ballast is carefully sprinkled in place before being pressed into the glue using a small wooden stick. On a ground level line ballasting can be done using a cement/sand/ballast mix which is applied dry before being wetted using a watering can fitted with a fine rose. So whatever track/ballast combination you decide on it is very much each to their own, and after all we are after the essence of trains running through a garden landscape rather than finescale modelling.

For a raised layout the extra building work can seem

Above
Dick Allan built his substantial Gauge 3 garden railway system at ground level, but he found that the track cleaning required for the DCC-controlled locomotives was physically quite demanding. Therefore he switched to a combination of battery-operated radio-control and live-steam propulsion, thus alleviating the need for rail cleaning.

CONSTRUCTING A RAISED TRACKBED

The accompanying diagram shows the method of construction for the raised trackbed supports on Lincaster, a Gauge 1 system built by Graham Nicholas that runs from his garage and around his garden. The methods outlined here are equally applicable to O gauge and Gauge 3 systems, with the dimensions adjusted to suit.

The raised trackbed for the outdoor sections are supported on posts spaced at 4' intervals; as a base Graham used Metposts (obtainable from DIY outlets), these being driven 2' down into the ground with a sledgehammer. A suitable length of 3" x 3" treated fencing post was then hammered into the holder of the Metpost. Four supports were completed in this manner before going back and levelling them – the datum for this being the exit height of the trackbed from the garage.

Marine ply was used for all the top boards, these being 8" wide for single track and 12" for double. Placed on top of the two adjacent supports, the ply was marked to the exact length (and angle, if curvature was involved). After sawing, 2" x 1" battening was glued and screwed to the longitudinal edges of the underside and the completed board was then given four coats of creosote.

Prior to fixing to the support, a length of

An overall view of *Lincaster*, showing clearly the construction methods employed. *Photo: Derek Shore*

2" x 1", cut 2" shorter than the top board, was screwed to the top of the facing aspect of the support. The top board then fitted snugly over this tee piece and was secured to the top of the support with 3" screws.

With the top boards in place across the four supports, it was time to repeat the process with the next section, until the trackbed was completed. Minor adjustments

were made as Graham went along to correct the level as required.

Prior to laying the track, the tops of the boards were covered with mineral felt. Then, with the track pinned in place, the felt was trimmed back to ballast shoulder width.

To keep the trackbed in good condition, all exposed parts of the top boards are treated with creosote twice a year.

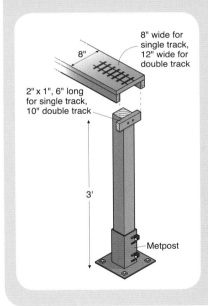

8" wide for single track, 12" wide for double track

8"

2" x 1", 6" long for single track, 10" double track

3'

Metpost

Close-up views of the foundations. The 3"x 3" supports are secured in Metposts driven into the ground. The top boards locate on tee-pieces. *Photos by Derek Shore*

daunting, and to some will look like trains running on stilts, but by careful planning even this can be incorporated into the overall scene. Adding bridges in strategic places adds a feeling of the layout being part of the landscape, and the use of slow growing hedging (such as Euonymus or Box hedging) will hide the structure.

Laying the track

It is important to ensure that the track is well laid, to avoid expensive locomotives and stock from derailing and being damaged. A usual starting place for tracklaying would be at a point or group of points with the plain track being laid away from this area, fixing the track as you go. It is helpful

to make some preset radii wooden curves to assist with laying curves, and these can be made from offcuts of plywood or hardboard, using a simple pencil and string approach to draw out the required radii. Cutting the curve is best done using a jigsaw. Before you start laying curved sections of track it is helpful to pre-curve some pieces of flexible track so that you can avoid dogleg joints where one piece of curved track joins to another.

Being outdoors, the rails will expand and contract with varying temperatures so it is important to leave a gap between the rail ends at every joint for expansion room (approx. 2mm for O gauge up to 3mm for Gauge 3). Tightly butting the rail ends together is to be avoided, because when the rails expand on a sunny day the track has nowhere to go except up or sideways which will inevitably lead to derailments and a lot of extra work to put things right.

One other thing to check as you are laying the track is the level across the rails; a short pocket size spirit level can be used for this, the aim being to have the straight track perfectly level with the bubble of the level bang in the middle. For curves it is useful to introduce a small amount of cant or superelevation so that the train leans into the curve for a smoother run – with the outer rail on curves raised above the inner rail by approx. 1mm. To keep the track in this position, small squares of styrene sheet can be used as packing under the outer sleeper ends.

Points are usually operated by hand, but some modellers do operate them using a 'wire-in-tube' arrangement or with electrically powered point motors.

Essential wiring outdoors

If you are using conventional track-powered locos you will need to connect up a controller to the track to do this. However, mains-powered controllers are not suitable for outdoor use. Many modellers will have a garden shed next to the layout to which mains power has been connected, and so the controller can be housed in there to keep it dry and safe.

Low voltage power from the controller to the track can be connected using multistrand wire of at least 16/0.2mm size, but ideally larger, with the track connection being a soldered one. The rail joiners outdoors are really only the physical connection and should not be relied upon for electrical continuity so a loop of wire needs to be soldered across at every rail joiner to give reliable connection of track power to all parts of the layout. Even points should be wired in this way to increase electrical reliability.

The rail head will tarnish just as the rest of the rail will do, and whilst this will give a pleasing, weathered effect to the rail as a whole, it will not allow good electrical pick up

by the locomotive through the wheels, so it will be necessary to clean the rail head surface with a track cleaning rubber (such as a Peco PL-41 track rubber) to impart a shine so that trains can run. Obviously for battery-powered or live-steam models, this consideration is academic.

Live steam and radio control

Many modellers employing live steam traction opt to run their engines under manual control, i.e. raise steam, hook up a rake of stock and set the train going at a steady pace while they sit back with a brew to enjoy the sights and sounds as the train proceeds around their railway. However this only really works successfully on a line that is both level and has generous radius curves; otherwise the locomotives can sometimes stall on the curves if they do not have a sufficient head of steam, or are running just a bit too slowly, meaning that the 'hand from the sky' has to intervene.

Employing radio control, however, allows you to be in constant control of your locomotive, plus it will allow you to stop at stations to collect passengers, or to indulge in a spot of shunting in the goods yard. The addition of r/c is relatively inexpensive and will convert a manual locomotive into a driveable machine, with

Above
Dick Allan demonstrating the use of radio control on his Gauge 3 system. This is a popular control method for the larger scales, there being ample space within the locomotive models to accommodate the batteries.

Below
Tony Crouch uses a Digitrax DCC system, with 'walkaround' sockets housed in ice cream containers. Lids protect them when not in use, and they are removed during the winter months.

Left
All the buildings and lineside details on *Combe Down* are placed *in situ* for operating sessions – only the fibreglass platforms are left in place all year round.

OPERATING GAUGE 1 LIVE STEAM LOCOMOTIVES

The fleet of locomotives which are run on Combe Down (by father and son team Don and John Froud) are all meths-fired live-steam models, manually controlled.

In readiness for an operating session – and as with full size practice – each locomotive is oiled, including filling a lubricator chamber, which provides steam oil to the cylinders when running.

The tender is filled with water and a hand pump used to fill the boiler via a clack valve. The fuel tank is filled with methylated spirit and a valve is opened to feed the burners (which works on the 'chicken feed' principle). The burners are then lit and an electric fan is placed in the chimney to help draw the fire.

When a suitable pressure is reached the fan is dispensed with and the blower valve is used to continue drawing the fire. As working pressure is reached (40 to 50psi) the regulator can be cracked open, helping to clear any condensate from cylinders and making the locomotive ready to take over

A close-up view of the cab controls in a Great Western Dean Goods 0-6-0.

the train. With the regulator open and blower closed, the train gets under way; a few judicious adjustments are made in the early stages of the run to achieve the speed required.

For engines provided with an axle-driven pump the supply of water to the boiler can be regulated, but if this is not the case occasional stops are made to use the hand

John tends to GWR Saint 4-6-0 No.2953 during a running session, having just topped up the tender with water.

pump to top up. When stopped the blower is opened to ensure the fire continues to draw and pressure maintained.

At the end of the run the tender is emptied of water and fuel, condensate is removed from the lubricator and steam oil residue is wiped off the model.

Perhaps surprisingly, there's little maintenance required to keep the loco fleet running smoothly; the boilers are cleaned occasionally with citric acid and the burners re-wicked. Piston rings and bearings need replacing from time to time, but essentially that's all the maintenance required. However, being live steam, the boilers each require a certificate of conformance and an annual safety inspection. (Guidance on these procedures is provided through the Gauge 1 Model Railway Association and further information is also available on its website – see Chapter 10.)

GWR Saint 4-6-0 No.2953, pictured at speed during a running session.

the option of forward or reverse at the flick of a stick on the r/c controller. This will make the loco more suited to sharply curved parts of the track, but also where a line has gradients.

Lineside details and structures

For buildings that live outdoors you will need those which are made in plastic or resin. However, many of the structure and lineside accessory kits that are commercially available, particularly for 7mm, are designed specifically for use on indoor layouts, and may not be suited to outdoor applications where they will be exposed to the extremeties of the British weather. One option is to keep many of the smaller details removable, so that they can be stored safely in the dry, and placed *in situ* for running sessions. This is

the approach taken by Don and John Froud for their Gauge 1 system *Combe Down*; all the buildings, fences, figures, lamps are removable and it takes about two hours to set up the railway for a running session.

And finally...

It is of course important to remember that your valuable locomotives and stock should be safely and securely stored. Although the passenger and goods stock can be locked away in a shed or garage, it is always advisable to store locomotives indoors, not only because of their value, but also to protect the steam powered ones from frost, as ice in a loco boiler could cause irreparable damage.

Above all though, garden railway modelling is intended to be both enjoyable and fun!

Matthew Cousins utilised the space available in his garden to create this 30' x 25' 7mm scale homage to the LNER, which comprises a double-track continuous run that passes through a purpose-built summer house – the indoor section featuring a fully-detailed wayside station.

The outside sections of trackbed were fabricated from UPVC fascia boards, fitted to carefully levelled supports of either timber or concrete construction. The surfaces of the fascia boards were covered with resin bonded pea beach, with Peco track then being laid on top and ballasted to suit. Rail joins were 'hard wired' to ensure durability.

The impressive replica of Victoria Bridge was fabricated from aluminium by one of Matthew's friends, and is demountable to allow ease of access to the central operating area and summer house. Operation is with analogue 12V dc.

An A4 rolls across the impressive bridge, whilst in the background a V2 sets back 'wrong line' from the station with a rake of Pullmans.

The summer house is loosely styled on a signal box and features ex-LBSC brackets from Faygate signal box.

The bridge can be lifted clear for ease of access to the summer house when the railway is not in use.

A J15 0-6-0 exits the summer house for a lap of the outdoor section. The apertures are closed off when the railway is not in use.

Sequence of construction

An overall view showing masonry work in progress to create the raised trackbed – the datum level being determined by the track height of the indoor section passing through the summer house.

The surface of the masonry was covered with strips of UPVC fascia board to form the foundation for the trackbed.

A layer of resin bonded pea beach aggregate was then added. The section illustrated is supported on levelled timber posts.

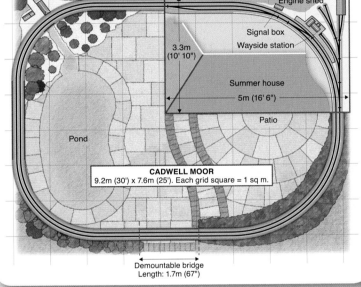

Track was laid next, fixed in place using more of the resin adhesive used to secure the pea beach.

Engine shed

Signal box
Wayside station

3.3m
(10' 10")

Summer house

5m (16' 6")

Patio

Pond

CADWELL MOOR
9.2m (30') x 7.6m (25'). Each grid square = 1 sq. m.

Demountable bridge
Length: 1.7m (67")

Soon after applying the resin, O gauge ballast was sprinkled on top, working on short sections at a time, excess ballast being brushed off after the resin had set. Note the wall sections added along the edges of the trackbed.

A J71 0-6-0T runs through the station that forms part of the indoor section housed in the summer house.

Chapter 12

Overseas O Scale modelling

In most of the world, modelling in O gauge is a relatively specialist area, currently representing perhaps 5% of the market (compared to 75-80% for HO). However, this was not always the situation, and there are signs that overseas O scale modelling is enjoying a resurgence.

Originally introduced by German toy manufacturer Märklin around 1900, as a smaller and cheaper alternative to Gauge 1, it should strictly be known as 'zero' or 'nought' (as indeed it is in French and German). Its popularity declined in Europe before the Second World War due to the introduction of smaller scales such as HO (the H signifying 'half'). In the USA the depression wiped out demand for expensive larger trains, and by 1932 O was the standard. Powered by three-rail alternating current, O gauge was the most common size for model railroads there until the early 1960s.

It is probably true to say that O had its heyday when model railways were considered toys, with more emphasis on robust construction and the capacity to be handled and operated easily by children. Accuracy and detail to create a realistic model were secondary concerns for commercial producers.

O scale overseas

Above
The magnificent Lenz model of the German standard BR50 2-10-0.

Below
Ahrtalzweibrück by John Illingworth is an excellent example of what can be achieved. Locos and stock seen here are all by Lenz. The layout featured in CONTINENTAL MODELLER in September 2012 and May 2018.
Photo: Derek Shore

In the USA, brands such as Ives, American Flyer, and Lionel used O gauge for their budget lines, in contrast to Gauge 1 premium products. As the trains were seen as toys, it was not important to use a consistent scale. Early Marx and other entry-level trains, usually made of lithographed tinplate, were not scaled at all but just made to convenient proportions. Yet these products ran on the same track, and, depending on the manufacturer, could sometimes be coupled together and run as part of the same train.

Post-war moves towards greater accuracy
After the Second World War, manufacturers started paying more attention to scale, and locomotives and rolling stock became more accurate in dimensions and more realistic in detail than earlier products.

A scale ratio of 1:43.5 was adopted in France and The Netherlands (the same as in Britain), while Germany and Switzerland opted for 1:45. 1:48 (¼" to the foot) is used in America.

The sheer bulk of the models can be impressive and attractive, but this poses problems in terms of the space required, and the growth of smaller scales – HO, TT, and N, better suited to the average domestic situation – saw O relegated to specialist status, largely the preserve of those who could afford museum quality limited edition metal models. Suppliers included such firms as Wunder, Kiss, Dingler, Micro-Metakit, Kauth, Demko, Hegob, Hobby-Technik,

OVERSEAS O SCALE MODELING 115

WMK, Apolda, Kesselbauer, Hehl, Hermann (Switzerland), Creanorm (Switzerland), and Swedtram (Sweden). Some of these companies developed considerable ranges, others dabbled but did not prosper. Some are still in business.

Further, both Rivarossi and Lima attempted mass produced plastic models.

European O in the 21st century

Developments in the past 15 years or so have made O popular with scale modellers who appreciate the level of detail and operational characteristics that can be achieved. Since the early 1990s, manufacturers have been placing more emphasis on realism, and O has experienced a resurgence. In Germany, the situation was changed dramatically by the entry of digital specialist Lenz into the market in 2006, with accurate and detailed plastic-bodied models and high-tech digital equipment for control, drive, lights, smoke, sound, etc. as standard. They have been followed by Brawa and MBW, with smaller concerns such as Schnellenkamp and O Scale Models (the latter is no longer active) providing rolling stock and accessories.

NMJ offers a small range of high quality Norwegian and

Swedish models, mostly in metal, while Heljan has produced the iconic Nohab diesel with a plastic body.

REE has some French items, with more planned.

Philotrain (Netherlands), Brassline (France), Proto Models (Italy), and Top Train (Italy) have created limited edition metal models.

Other suppliers of limited edition high quality brass models such as Fulgurex, Lematec (formerly Lemaco), and Elettren also offers O scale models for various markets.

Structures and lineside details

Many of the companies producing laser-cut structure kits offer O scale versions – these include Joswood, Moebo, Bünnig, Real-Modell, and Stangel. Other German small suppliers include: Hofmanns, Waller, PTM (Präzisionstechnik und Modellbau), Lehmann Modellbau, Hansen Trains (accessories), and Hauser (figures).

In addition, Preiser (figures) and Ladegüter Bauer (loads) offer some O scale products.

Structures, scenic materials, and accessories suitable for

Top left
A Lenz DB VT98 railbus on *Klinkerhofen*, built by the Raven family. CM September 2016.

Top right
Lenz has developed a model of the BR89 (former Prussian T3) 0-6-0T.

Above
A DB V200 B-B diesel (by MBW) comes off its train at *Höchstädt*, built by Bill Bishop. CM May 2015.

Below
Bern Lötschberg Simplon Ae6/8 electric, a limited edition brass model by Fulgurex.

Philotrain specialises in limited edition models for the Dutch market.

Above
NS 500/600 class 0-6-0 diesel shunter.

Right
NS 2200 class diesel.
Photo: Philotrain

Above
A Wiener Stadtbahn
four-wheel coach
made by BuBi-Modell.

Above right
A SOO Line F unit
(an old Atlas model)
on *Pipestem Creek*
built by Alan Whitney.
CM January 2011.

Right
Outside the loco depot
on *Pipestem Creek*.
This level of detail is
typical of O scale.

Below
Great Northern H4
Pacific and O8 2-8-2
at Boundary Springs
on the *Columbia and
Western* layout, set in
Canada in the 1950s,
built by Mike Dobson.
CM May, July, August,
and September 2018.

O are also available from some of the well-known brands – for example, Busch, Noch, Heki, etc.

Support for European O
The sector is supported by *Spur Null Magazin* and *012 Magazin* (both in German). There is a dedicated O scale exhibition each year in Germany in early March, originally in Buseck and now in nearby Giessen.

Vintage O gauge
Collecting vintage O gauge trains is quite popular, and there is a market for both original and reproduction models. Names active in this area include ETS, a concern from the Czech Republic which produces robust metal-bodied locos and stock with sophisticated electronics for sound and control. Merkur is another Czech manufacturer of tinplate-like O gauge toy trains (two or three rail, with or without sound); BuBi-Modell (also Czech) includes some models for O while Paya from Spain offers 'retro' products.

The European and American prototypes produced for MTH are distributed in Europe by Busch. They were initially more in the toy tradition but latterly have become more realistic.

American O
The market for North American O scale is quite large with a fair selection of locomotives and freight cars available, covering a wide range of periods and prototypes. They are modelled in 1:48 (¼" to the foot) scale.

Fine and coarse track standards have been adopted by modellers, the latter sometimes using three-rail ac.

Left
Columbia & Western: Canadian Pacific #8912 is a Fairbanks-Morse 'Trainmaster', made from a K-Line three-rail model, with much modified body, extra pick-ups, LED lights, and a DCC decoder.

Below
Emerging from the upper storage loops onto the trestle is Great Northern M2 2-6-8-0 #1981, a Sunset brass model converted to DCC with extra pickups and LED lighting.

Foot of page
This Victorian Railways Diesel Electric Rail Motor (DERM) is a metal model made for The Haskell Company.

The history of O scale in America is complicated, with products having been transferred between owners and brand names over time. However, the main suppliers of American O scale trains currently are Atlas, Lionel, MTH, and Weaver. Other brands include Williams (three-rail ac, now part of Bachmann), and Bachmann (some structures and accessories).

In the past many small firms were involved, including AMT/KMT, K-Line, Ives, Marx, Sakai, and others.

Most of the brass importers have offered O scale models; among them Custom Brass, Kemtron, Key Imports, KTM, MMI, Overland, Pacific Fast Mail, Precision Scale Models, Sunset, and Westside. (Some of these are still active.)

Australian O scale

O in Australia is a very small section of the market but has been growing in recent years. The production of local prototypes seems to be a flourishing cottage industry.

Suppliers (large and small) include Andlan Models, Auscision, Bergs Hobbies, Haskell, Ixion, Kieran Ryan, Model O Kits, and Outback Model Company.

Further information

CONTINENTAL MODELLER frequently features O gauge layouts and models from all over the world. European and American products are also readily available from selected specialist retailers in Britain, many of which advertise in this monthly publication.

Chapter 13

Track plans for O gauge and above

I n contrast to the smaller scales, it is surprising that there have been few specifically O gauge track plan books – although to be fair the traditional Freezer publications gave equivalent dimensions on the nominally 1' grid squares. The pages that follow illustrate plans large and small with the crucial advantage of actually having been built; adjusting the scale of a plan might not take into account the required clearances for lineside structures, mid-coach overhangs and so on.

Inevitably, most of the plans are for relatively modest schemes; moving up to 7mm scale doesn't suddenly double the amount of space you have available for your project! As mentioned in Chapter 6, it is perfectly possible to combine bullhead Peco Streamline code 124 trackwork with the recently released Setrack – for off-stage sections, fiddle yards etc – as the sectional track uses the same profile rail. (Remember too that Peco produces a transition track, ref.SL-713, to link code 124 and the code 143 flat-bottom trackwork, so if your chosen period needs the more modern flat-bottom format the Setrack will still have its off-stage uses.)

We have included a couple of 'pipe dream' plans in the layout gallery chapter, such as *Bucks Hill*, but there's a couple here too. Those tempted to try Gauge 3 beware: the classic Great Western branch terminus as shown by *St Ives*, is around 88' long, and made up of 22 baseboards each of which is 4' square! Gauge 3 is *big…*

Dormston Terminus (O)

This layout by Stephen Shepherd (pictured on p40) is a compact interpretation of the branch line terminus concept, which here comprises four points and features a run-round loop – all contained a scenic section just 7' long. Train lengths are restricted – the loop can accommodate either a single bogie coach or three wagons – but the plan enables the key shunting moves to be completed 'on scene'. The layout is housed along the wall of Stephen's railway room.

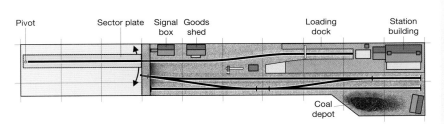

Overall dimensions: 10' 0" x 1' 3". Each grid square =1ft x 1ft.

St Georges Dock (O)

With a scenic section measuring only slightly more than 6' x 4', this dockside layout (built by Alan Gray) occupies a similar footprint to that of the archetypal 'table-top' setup in OO. It is an ideal candidate for utilising items from the Peco O gauge bullhead Setrack range, inset to suit. Note that the scenic section is designed to be viewed from two sides, which adds further interest to the finished layout.
The scheme provides a suitable setting for a stud of small locomotive types (such as the Minerva Peckett E Class 0-4-0ST and Victory Class 0-6-0T), together with a multitude of four-wheel wagons; covered vans, opens and tanks etc.

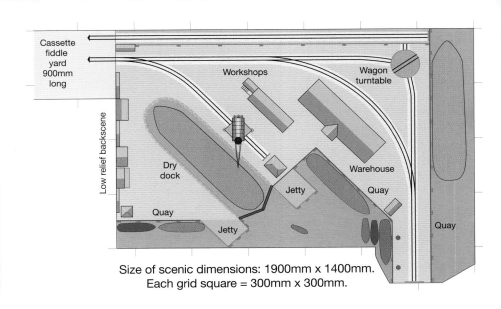

Size of scenic dimensions: 1900mm x 1400mm.
Each grid square = 300mm x 300mm.

Arun Quay (O)

This stunning 7mm scale essay by master modeller Gordon Gravett (illustrated on p6) depicts a rural rail-served quayside, with small kitbuilt 0-6-0Ts as the staple motive power; namely a Stroudley Terrier – which has since been made available as an R-T-R model by Dapol – and a Wainwright P Class. With the operation entirely focused on the shunting of freight stock, the Alex Jackson method of remote uncoupling has been employed (see p46).

The careful placement of buildings and structures acts as a visual foil for the extremities of the scenic section, which measures a very compact 7'6" x 1'9". Only a modest-sized turntable fiddle yard is required to accommodate trains comprising one of the small tank engines and no more than a handful of wagons.

Overall scenic dimensions:
7' 6" x 1' 9", plus fiddle yard.
Each grid square = 1ft x 1ft.

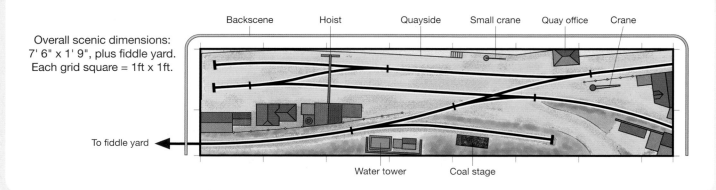

To fiddle yard

Backscene · Hoist · Quayside · Small crane · Quay office · Crane

Water tower · Coal stage

Selsey Town (O)

Keith Smith devised an L-shaped plan for the basis of this model of a light railway (see p41). Although constructed as a portable exhibition layout, the configuration is quite adaptable for home use, arranged around two walls of a room. To reduce the size of the plan, the disused branch line could be dispensed with to turn the plan into a terminus to fiddle yard arrangement, whilst the section of running line between the station throat and fiddle yard could be reduced.

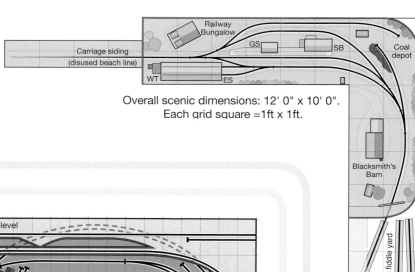

Overall scenic dimensions: 12' 0" x 10' 0".
Each grid square =1ft x 1ft.

Chadbury (O)

Eric Bottomley managed to squeeze a double-track mainline continuous run into a footprint of just 17' x 17' – the dimensions of his converted double-garage space. Achieving this necessitated extensive use of curved pointwork and Peco code 124 bullhead flexible plain track – the main running lines featuring no straight sections whatsoever.

Note the two raised lines, which operate on an automated shuttle. The central area of the layout is accessed through a doorway crossed by the removable girder bridge pictured on p38.

Although Eric's layout depicts an industrialised Midlands town, the scheme could easily be interpreted as a rural setting.

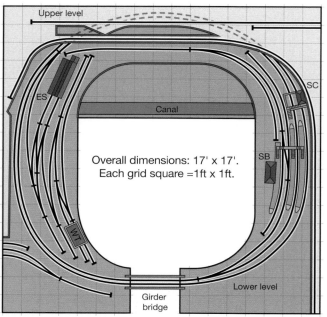

Overall dimensions: 17' x 17'.
Each grid square =1ft x 1ft.

Netherwood Sidings (O)

Graham Clark's tribute to the Woodhead Route (pictured on p40) encompasses an area of 33' x 11'6" in full exhibition trim. However, the modular format of the scenic and fiddle yard boards means that the length can be reduced slightly to enable a smaller configuration to be accommodated in Graham's attic for operation at home. The plan features a double-track main line running along the front of the scenic section, with a 'half yard' situated behind, which is disguised with a bridge running across the severed ends of the siding lines. The scheme is ideal for modellers who enjoy running main line length trains and also have a particular passion for freight stock!

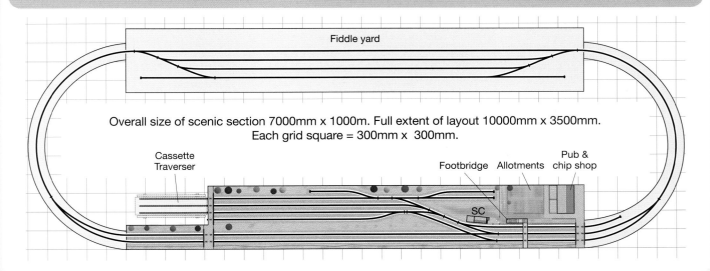

Overall size of scenic section 7000mm x 1000m. Full extent of layout 10000mm x 3500mm.
Each grid square = 300mm x 300mm.

St. Petroc (G1)

Constructed by John Green and Tony Massey of the Sheffield Model Railway Enthusiasts, St. Petroc proves that a viable Gauge 1 scheme can be devised in a very modest space. This compact branch terminus (pictured on p100) is based on Bodmin General, but with an island platform added to increase the operational interest. In spite of its small size the platform can accommodate a GWR small Prairie and two B-set coaches. The 6' fiddle yard does add considerably to the overall length, but restricting the train lengths further will enable a much smaller fiddle yard to be used.

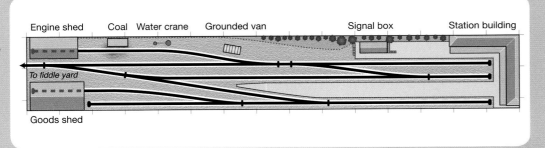

St. Ives (G3)

As alluded to in the introduction to this chapter, a workable scheme in Gauge 3 commands a lot of space; this classic branch line terminus arrangement is a case in point, scaling out at a staggering 88' in length. As presented, however, there is plenty of scope for compression – the length of the scenic section could be all-but-halved if the viaduct and engine shed were to be omitted from the plan.

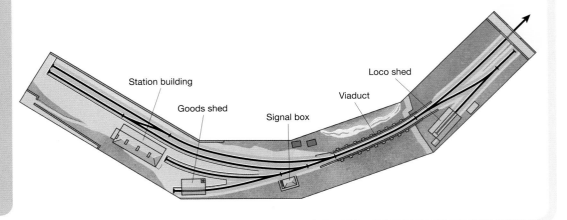

Acknowledgements

This publication would not have been possible without the modelling input of the following, some of whom are sadly no longer with us.

Dick Allan, Paul Bambrick, Andrew Beard, Geoff Bigmore, Bill Bishop, Eric Bottomley, Maurice Bramley, Jack Burnard, Vincent Caldwell, Peter Callon & friends, Graham Clark, Trevor Collins, Matthew Cousins, Tony Crouch, Mike Dobson, Norman Eagles & 'gang', Andrew Forty, Cyril Freezer, Don & John Froud, Cyril Fry, Ian Futers, members of the Gainsborough Model Railway Society, Gordon & Maggie Gravett, Alan Gray, John Green, Dave Hall, Pat Hammond, James Harrison, Michael Heaven & friends, members of the Hillingdon Railway Modellers, Col R J Hoare, John Illingworth, David Jenkinson, Pete Martin, Tony Massey, Don Neale, members of Newport MRS, Graham Nicholas, members of the North Devon O Gauge Group, Peter Osbourne, Mike Perry, Marc Pretious, Sydney Pritchard, the Raven family, Alan Searle, Stephen Shepherd, Keith Smith, Richard Spoors, members of Swindon MRC, Ian Thompson, Simon Thompson, Chris Thorp, Tim Tincknell, Dave Walker, Pete Waterman, Michael Watts, Martyn Welch, Kevin Wilson, Alan Whitney, members of Yeovil MRG.

Bibliography & Further Reading

Your Guide to Railway Modelling & Layout Construction
Peco Publications, ref.PM-200
– second edition published in 2015
ISBN 978-0900586 00 2

2018 Peco Catalogue
Includes all the Peco Group products, incorporating Parkside kits

The Peco Modellers' Library Compendium of Track Plans
Peco Publications, ref.PM-202
published in 2015
ISBN 0 9000586 02 6

60 Plans for Small Locations
Peco Publications, ref.PB-3

Peco 'Shows You How' booklets:
SYH1 Layout Planning & Design
SYH2 Building Baseboards
SYH4 Wiring the Layout – part 1, first steps (revised edition September 2016)
SYH17 Introducing DCC
SYH19 Railway Modelling Outdoors
SYH25 Introducing DCC Sound

Ramsay's Model Train Guide 9th edition
Compiled by Pat Hammond
(Warners Group Publications)

The Bassett-Lowke Story by
Roland Fuller (New Cavendish Books)

Model Railways and their builders by
Jack Ray (Atlantic Transport Publishers)

James Stanley Beeson by
R A Ganderton (Faculty Publishing)

Hornby – the official illustrated history
by Ian Harrison with Pat Hammond
(Harper Collins)

British Toy Trains by
Michael D Foster (published by author)

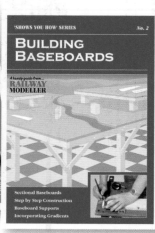

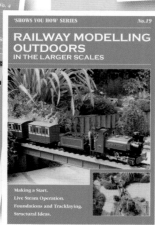

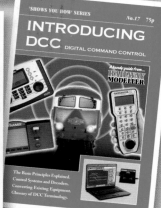